THE
BREADMAN'S
HEALTHY BREAD
·B·O·O·K·

THE BREADMAN'S HEALTHY BREAD ·B·O·O·K·

Use Your Bread Machine to Make More Than 100 Delicious, Wholesome Breads

George Burnett

WILLIAM MORROW AND COMPANY, INC.

New York

Library of Congress Cataloging-in-Publication Data
Burnett, George.
        The breadman's healthy bread book: use your bread machine to make more than 100 delicious, wholesome breads / George Burnett.
            p. cm.
        Includes bibliographical references and index.
        ISBN 0-688-12025-3
        1. Bread.   2. Cookery (Cereals)   3. Automatic bread machines.
    I. Title.
    TX769.B88   1992
    641.8'15—dc20   92-25402
                                                                                    CIP

Printed in the United States of America

First Edition

                9 10

BOOK DESIGN BY GIORGETTA BELL McREE

To my sweetheart
and loving wife, Christy

ACKNOWLEDGMENTS

There are so many inspirational and wonderful people in my life. I owe a lot to Rick Cesari at Trillium Health Products for believing in me and giving me the opportunity to share my nutritional convictions nationally.

To Steve Cesari and Bob Lamson at Trillium Health Products for their constant support and encouragement.

To a true friend, Ann Zinn, for her continuing belief in me.

To Gerald Koblentz, part of the Breadman Team at Trillium, thanks.

To the outstanding seminar coordinators: Heather, Lauren, Katie, Bobbie, Jana, Jane, Geri, and Siun. Also to the great staff members who made the hundreds of seminars across the nation successful—thanks for all your hard work.

To the nutritional staff for their thorough research and constant help: Brenda, Daniella, Kristen, and Barbara. And to Lara Pizzorno. A big thanks to the entire Trillium team in Seattle. You are the greatest!

Thanks to Will Schwalbe, my editor at William Morrow and Company, for his enthusiastic spirit and belief in this project. Also to his assistant Zachary Schisgal, thank you!

A tremendous thanks to Jericho Promotions for their past and ongoing public relations work. Thank you Eric, Jon, Sherri, Beverly, Ellen, Todd, and Kim.

I wish to give a huge thank you to Mary Goodbody for her long hours of wonderful help with the text and her much appreciated editorial assistance in the preparation of the manuscript. And thanks also to Mary Dauman for her help editing the recipes.

To Rick Rodgers and his staff for their expertise in testing and re-testing all the recipes to perfection. Rick, you are a culinary genius. Thanks!

To my assistants, Linda Shaw and Merrill Morgan, thank you so much.

And also thanks to Pat Cunninghan, for your help.

Thank you to my friend Charles McQuire, a cereal chemist at Montana State University, for his advice over the years that has helped me so much with my recipes.

Thanks to my former employees and customers of Burnett's Stone-ground Bakery and also to Bill Larson for sharing his years of baking expertise. Thanks to you all!

To Patti Rowles, a longtime bread-making friend. Thanks for all your valuable input.

To the Folkvords at Montana Wheat Bakery for continuing with my bakery's original goal of producing whole-grain breads commercially.

To Susan Cesari for her friendship and support during my early days with Trillium.

To the memory of Lou Jonas for taking an interest in me as a young boy and teaching me about nature, particularly wild edible plants.

Also to the memory of Christy's parents, Eldon and Eunice Nielsen, thanks for all they did raising a great daughter for me to marry. Mom Nielson always had a sincere interest in my success.

My deepest gratitude to my parents, Darwin and Barbara Burnett, for their dedication to my two brothers, Tom and Ross, my six beautiful sisters, Rhyll Ann, Del Raye, Marta, Shauna, Dawn, and Heidi, and to me. My parents taught us all about health and provided the foods that have kept us healthy and vibrant today. Dad and Mom are still a great inspiration and example for staying active and productive. Their example could inspire anyone. I love you both very much!

A special thank you to my wife, Christy, to whom this book is dedicated, and to our four handsome sons, Benjamin, Isaac, Niel, and Matthew. They are my reason for wanting to stay healthy and strong. They put up with a lot during my seminar travels and during the early days of the bakery when Ben took his naps on sacks of flour. Thank you for hanging in there with me!

Last, my sincere gratitude to the thousands of people who attend my seminars and apply the principles of health and nutrition to their daily lives. Thank you for the stories of success. Good luck, stay healthy, dare to dream, and to make your dreams come true!

CONTENTS

INTRODUCTION

The best way to guarantee that you and your family get the very best food is to make it yourself. This is so easy with the bread machine it is almost magical. In the privacy of your own kitchen *you* combine the flour and water, *you* add the yeast, *you* select the sweetener (if any), and *you* push the button to start the baking process. That's all there is to it! And at the end of the cycle you have an aromatic loaf of fresh-as-can-be bread bursting with the goodness of whole grains and containing no hidden additives or refined sugar.

I firmly believe in eating whole grains, and you will come to understand why as you read this book. Their nutritional benefits are manifold. Have you seen the new Food Pyramid developed by the federal government? The bottom portion, from which we are meant to eat the most, lists whole grains. Getting enough whole grains is no problem when you make it a habit to eat breads made with whole-grain flours. Flours made from grains such as whole wheat and rye make better-tasting and more nutritious breads than those made from standard, nutritionally depleted all-purpose, or so-called bread, flour.

At first, you may be surprised by the flavor of these breads, especially if you are not accustomed to whole-grain foods. A friend who tried my recipe for 100 Percent Whole Wheat Bread (see page 66) called me with a less-than-enthusiastic reaction. It tastes okay, he said, but it's a little chewy and not at all sweet. How about adding a little shortening and sugar?

Absolutely not!

The whole-grain breads I espouse are made without shortening and refined white sugar. Occasionally, I sweeten a loaf with barley malt, molasses, fruit juice, or honey, or add fruit and nuts for interesting texture and taste, but I never compromise my beliefs by catering to America's collective desire for sweet, fatty foods.

We have distorted our taste buds with all the processed foods we eat. When a child grows up believing the soft, mushy, white supermarket brand is *bread*, how is he or she supposed to react to a slice of chewy, robust whole wheat bread? It tastes foreign at first. I understand this, but the great news is that it quickly begins to taste *right*—as well as indescribably delicious.

This is what I hope you get from this book. The breads you make with the following recipes and an automatic bread maker should, after a few weeks, taste so glorious that you will never want to go back to the old way.

The bread machine makes this feasible. There it sits on the counter, waiting for you to measure out the flour and push the button. That's all you do. Walk away from it and when you return, the bread is baked and ready for cooling and slicing. Easy, isn't it? There is no reason to knead the dough, wait for two risings, and then heat an oven for the final baking. All you do is combine the ingredients in the bread pan in the order specified in the recipe or for your particular machine (some have yeast dispensers, for instance; others require the yeast be added first—or last) and switch on the machine. You may decide to set the timer so that the bread is ready at a specified time, or you may want to start the kneading, rising, and baking cycles right away. The choice is yours.

The choice is also yours to alter your eating habits to include wholesome, nutritious whole-grain breads. If you are already doing so, this book will simply enlarge your recipe collection, show you the convenience of the bread machine, and make eating healthfully that much easier.

THE
BREADMAN'S
HEALTHY BREAD
·B·O·O·K·

THE GOODNESS OF WHOLE-GRAIN BREADS

Whole grains are high in fiber, a good source of complex carbohydrates, B-complex vitamins, and minerals. They contain valuable oils—and they are low in fat and cholesterol-free. Since I was a child I have eaten breads and other dishes made from whole grains, and I cannot imagine another diet. I also eat lots of fruits and vegetables, brown rice, and legumes.

Breads made from whole grains are dark and chewy. They taste full and rich and their texture is so different from the spongy, soft texture of store-bought bread you will think you have discovered a new food. The idea of such a discovery is not far from the truth. As far as I am concerned, the stuff the big food companies pack in elongated plastic bags and call "bread" is useless food made with vitamin-poor bleached white flour. Even when the label says "wheat flour" it means "white flour." Only when the ingredient list says "whole wheat flour" are you getting any whole-grain flour. To claim any food value at all, the flour has been "enriched" with four of the twenty-six essential nutrients stripped from it during the milling process in the first place! Read the label. You will see that the refined flour is enriched only with niacin, iron, thiamin, and riboflavin (part of the B complex). The *whole* grain originally had all four elements, plus twenty-two more. Why the consumer accepts this simply does not make any sense to me.

I absolutely believe you are what you eat. You may have heard that before, but I cannot emphasize it enough. If you eat healthful foods, chances are you will *be* healthy. If you load up on fats, sugars, and salty foods, how can you expect to feel energetic and healthy? You are more likely to feel sluggish and tired. And you may be overweight, suffering from heart disease or other chronic problems relating to obesity.

Have you noticed the correlation between the food in a shopping cart and the person pushing it through the supermarket aisles? Next time you shop, take a look. Carts overloaded with processed, fat-laden, salty, and sugary foods are all too often manned by overweight people. Carts stocked with fresh fruits and vegetables, whole-grain flour, and other wholesome foods frequently are pushed by lithe, healthy-looking folks. I know this is not categorically true, but I have witnessed what I call the "cart correlation" too many times to believe it to be simple coincidence.

THE SAD TRUTH ABOUT AMERICA'S HEALTH

My mission in this book is to educate people about the importance of whole grains. Complex carbohydrates provided by these grains are important for energy. The insoluble fiber provided by them helps our digestive systems work more efficiently; too many of us are constipated or suffer from other problems with regularity. Did you know that colo-rectal cancer is on the increase and accounts for nearly 70,000 deaths a year? The American Cancer Society says much of this cancer is diet-related. Nearly 500,000 other cancers diagnosed every year are affected by diet, too. What is more, every day about 2,000 Americans die of heart disease. The American Heart Association tells us that many complications of heart disease are diet-related, too.

What does this mean? Clearly, as a nation, we are not eating as healthfully as we could. Other countries have lower incidences of certain cancers and heart disease, not to mention other ailments, and very often researchers link these indications of good health to diet. Why don't we, as Americans, include more grains, vegetables, fruits, and other wholesome foods in our diets? Obviously, it would be good for us. Read Chapter 3, beginning on page 15, for in-depth information on the value of complex carbohydrates and fiber in the diet.

Making breads from whole grains is a terrific start to changing to a more heathful way of eating. With my recipes and the bread machine, it is easy, too. Of course, you should also make sure to eat lots of fresh fruits and vegetables and cut back on the empty calories in sugar and the dangerous ones in high-fat foods. Most of my recipes include only whole-grain flours and other healthful ingredients. I purposely omit refined sugar and processed, bleached white flour and limit fats such as butter and cheese.

THE DING DONG GENERATION

I am equally concerned about the health of American children. Too many are growing up eating poorly—even those from affluent families who can afford anything in the markets. These children are part of what I call the Ding Dong generation, youngsters who cram as much junk food into their bodies as they can. They zip around on "sugar highs," find it difficult to concentrate in school, and tend to be overweight and out of shape. And they are kids! They should be able to pay attention in class with sharp, flexible minds, feel full of energy on the playing field, and munch crisp apples and wholesome bread after school.

I am working toward educating this generation (and their parents) on the benefits of a healthful diet. Foods made from whole grains are excellent sources of nutrition. Coupled with fresh vegetables and a good supply of fruit, they provide growing, young bodies with energy and nourishment simply not available from Ding Dongs and potato chips. I want whole-grain bread and fresh juice to become the "milk and cookies" of the 1990s!

MY PERSONAL PHILOSOPHY FOR HEALTHFUL EATING

I have a theory I call the 70/30 rule. Seventy percent of the time make a point of eating as healthfully as you possibly can. Make whole-grain breads, organic produce, legumes, and fresh juices the focus of your daily diet. Forego refined sugar, bleached all-purpose flour, animal fats, dairy products, and meats. The rest of the time, approximately 30 percent of it, *try* to eat healthfully, but do not panic if you cannot.

Let me give you an example of how this might work. You have eaten healthfully all week and on Saturday night your aunt invites you for dinner. It's your cousin's birthday and your aunt spent all afternoon making the chocolate cake you and your cousin loved as kids. I certainly don't suggest you refuse a small slice of cake. Why hurt your aunt's feelings? There are times when other things are more important than the correct diet.

The key to maintaining a healthful diet and lifestyle is balance in all things. Eat sensibly but don't go overboard and upset your aunt or anyone else. When you find balance, you will eat better, be healthier, feel less stress, and find time for the activities that mean the most.

I have developed bread recipes with the 70/30 rule in mind. Approximately 70 percent of the recipes are for whole-grain breads without a trace of white all-purpose flour. I call these my ''elite'' recipes. The other 30 percent of the recipes have white and whole-grain flour. These are what I refer to as ''transition'' recipes—recipes designed to help you gradually make the leap from baking as you know it to baking with whole-grain flours exclusively.

The transition recipes call for whole-grain flours as well as *unbleached* all-purpose flour. The white flour makes them a little lighter and perhaps more familiar. You know where to find the sacks of white flour in the supermarket and will feel comfortable buying and using it. At the same time, start buying whole-grain flours in small quantities, either from the supermarket or natural food store, and begin experimenting with them by following the recipes beginning on page 56. Once you are accustomed to the taste and texture of these breads, I promise you will want to forge ahead and make the recipes that eliminate all white flour. These wholesome, nutritious breads, with their rich, earthy flavors and satisfyingly chewy textures, will become staples in your house and you will, as I do, shake your head in disbelief that anyone is satisfied with store-bought bread.

HOW I BEGAN BAKING

I grew up eating homemade dishes made from fresh foods. I have always lived in Montana, one of the world's most magnificent wheat-growing areas, and some of my earliest memories are of watching my parents grind grain into flour for our bread. I am not exaggerating: My mother was grinding wheat when she went into labor with me! Perhaps this was fate, and I was destined to grow up with a special love of whole grains and breads.

We ate natural foods because my parents believed in them. We also did so for economy. My father was a schoolteacher who had to provide for nine hungry children. The last things my folks could spend cash on were expensive premade or processed foods. I remember feeling embarrassed about taking a sandwich made with thick slices of whole wheat bread, vegetables, and sprouts to school. I hunkered down under my desk to eat my lunch, wishing that I had Wonder Bread and bologna like everyone else. But even at the height of such schoolboy foolishness, I knew deep down that I *preferred* the more wholesome food.

By the time I was in my teens I was baking alongside Mom. I learned a lot from her and began to understand that I wanted to devote my life to baking wholesome breads and spreading the word about the value of a good diet. I could not then, and I cannot today, understand how people can be oblivious to what they put in their mouths. We had a neighbor who was constantly running around with her large family, feeding the kids on-the-go suppers from Taco Bell and McDonald's. I remember when I was seventeen suggesting that she consider more healthful food for herself and her children. She said she would like to, but, gosh, she just did not have the time.

Today she is bedridden, suffering from a host of complaints, and she is only in her forties. She tells me she has changed her ways and is eating whole-grain breads, vegetables, and fruits and drinking lots of fresh juices. She feels better every week, and I hope she soon will be up and around. I truly believe her problems stem from a poor and unbalanced diet.

In 1978 my father and mother, Darwin and Barbara Burnett, opened a little bakery in our home in Bozeman. It did not surprise my sisters or me that everyone loved Mom's baking and four years later the family bakery's success meant a move to larger quarters in town. It was called Burnett's Bon Ton Bakery, after the building that housed it. Every morning my mother ground flour from Montana wheat for the whole wheat breads, rolls, and ever-popular cinnamon rolls. In the spring of 1984, my wife, Christy, and I bought out my parents, who were ready to slow down a little, and moved the bakery to a bigger location further down Main Street. We changed the name to Burnett's Stone Ground Bakery and began marketing our wholesome products to local restaurants and other businesses, as well as a legion of loyal retail customers. After a single year, we moved to still larger quarters on the edge of town.

I have since sold the bakery so I could concentrate on traveling around the country to spread the word on the goodness and the healthful properties of whole grains, but during the years Christy and I ran it, I learned a lot about baking. The more I bake, the more committed I am to grains, be they wheat, rye, buckwheat, amaranth, quinoa, spelt, or any of the others. I discuss the differences among these grains in Chapter 3 that begins on page 15. Regardless of your particular preference, eating bread made from the whole grain, not just the starchy endosperm that makes white flour, is markedly better for your body and, I think you will agree, your soul.

BREAD AS THE STAFF OF LIFE

Since the earliest days, bread has sustained mankind. Nearly every culture has a hearth bread, from the Mexican tortilla to the Middle Eastern pita. Ancient, nomadic tribes carried precious seeds of grain with them, tenderly planting and tilling the soil to ensure a good harvest wherever they stopped for more than a few nights. Often the grain-growing propensity of an area determined whether it was settled. In ancient times, Mesopotamia's fertile crescent was most likely the first major grain-growing region, and because of the life-giving crop, could emerge as the recognized cradle of civilization. When the abilities of yeast were realized, bread took on new dimensions and through the centuries man has been baking breads of all descriptions.

Gazing at the ageless natural beauty of my native Montana, I find myself contemplating how we, as a people, came from caring so much about the grain, its goodness and its ability to make life-giving bread, to the present.

Most wheat is milled into the bleached white all-purpose flour you buy, with nary a thought to its origin, in the local grocery store or supermarket. The rest is milled into flour for gigantic commercial bakeries which turn out millions of nutritionally bankrupt loaves of "white" bread every day. In fact, approximately 90 percent of all bread sold in the U.S. is the "enriched" variety.

HOW THE BREAD MACHINE
CAN HELP YOUR DIET

You do not have to eat bland, nutrient-robbed store-bought bread again. With the bread machine, you can have fresh, wholesome bread every day of your life. Use the recipes in this book, learn the ins and outs of the machine, and develop your own recipes, or use the mixes Trillium

Health Products devises, under my supervision, for quick, healthful breads. With these mixes, you add the water and turn on the machine. Simple! They provide the perfect amount of dry ingredients and pre-measured packets of yeast. At least 50 percent of each one is whole-grain flour and some are 100 percent whole grain. They contain no bromates, hydrogenated oils, or shortening. Trillium currently markets six wholesome and delicious varieties: Whole Wheat, Light Wheat, Caraway Rye, Cinnamon-Raisin, Carob Date Nut, and 7-Grain. See page 289 for ordering information.

I promise that after a month or so of relying on the machine you will find that you look forward to the bread as much or more than the sandwich filling; toast will be a new pleasure; and you will feel so good about the great food you are feeding yourself and your family you will never resort to store-bought bread again. Plus, you will notice a change in the weekly food bill. Although bread is not an expensive item, once you stock up on a few essential ingredients, making your own is far less costly than buying it. Perhaps most important, you and your family will feel better than ever before.

WHY WHOLE GRAINS ARE GOOD FOR YOU

Given the increased awareness nowadays about the benefits of complex carbohydrates and fiber, it's hard to believe that only decades ago we believed fiber was "wasted" food. As recently as the 1970s, most food companies processed foods to get rid of the fiber!

Too many Americans still eat this old-fashioned way, neglecting foods high in fiber and misunderstanding that complex carbohydrates are *good* for you. Many of us still think a healthful meal is a big steak and a green salad dripping with dressing. Nothing could be further from the truth.

The reality is that we should eat less meat, less fat, and less sodium. Instead we should eat more fruits, vegetables, legumes (such as dried beans and peas), and whole grains. These foods provide fiber and complex carbohydrates important for good health.

WHAT ARE COMPLEX CARBOHYDRATES?

The body needs carbohydrates for energy. They act as fuel to keep our brains, muscles, and internal organs functioning. Our bodies do not store most of the calories from carbohydrates—they store only the calories from fat!—and, therefore, we must replace these vital calories every day. The good news is that our bodies burn calories derived from carbohydrates efficiently and quickly. As too many of us know, this is not true of calories derived from fat. They are harder to burn.

What I find particularly telling is that both simple and complex carbohydrates have four calories per gram—exactly the same as protein. Fat, on the other hand, has nine calories per gram of weight.

Sugars—glucose, fructose, and sucrose—are simple carbohydrates and while we need these as much as the more complex carbohydrates, they are easy to come by. They are found in fruits and vegetables. We also consume simple carbohydrates when we eat refined sugars and syrups. Eating a balanced diet rich in fruits and vegetables provides the body with more than enough simple carbohydrates. There is no need to *add* refined sugar to anything.

Complex carbohydrates are all those foods we used to refer to as starches. Time was when "starch" was a bad word. If you went on a weight-reducing diet, the first thing you did was cut out starches such as breads and potatoes. What a mistake. These foods, which include grains and starchy vegetables, are essentially fat-free and cholesterol-free. They are rich in valuable vitamins and minerals, they fill you up without adding fat-laden calories, and they are terrific sources of dietary fiber. The vitamin most associated with whole grains is the B complex, a grouping that includes thiamin (B_1), riboflavin (B_2), and niacin (B_3). The B vitamins are essential for metabolizing complex carbohydrates so that the body receives the energy it needs. They contribute to maintaining a healthy cholesterol level, protect against some cancers, and contribute significantly to healthy skin and hair. Deficiencies are rare. The B complex vitamins are available in legumes, green leafy vegetables, sprouts, and nutritional yeast, as well as whole grains. Essential minerals, particularly calcium, iron, and zinc, also naturally occur in many whole grains and whole-grain flours—but are removed from all-purpose white flour during processing.

Today, nutritionists and some medical doctors alike recommend that everyone include ten or eleven servings a day of complex carbohydrates so that they comprise 55 to 60 percent of our total calories. This translates to four or five two- to three-ounce servings *every day* of fruits and vegetables, and five or six servings of whole grains and legumes.

Staying on this regimen is easy when you include whole-grain breads in your diet.

WHAT IS DIETARY FIBER?

Fiber is an essential element that, strange as it may sound, cannot be digested. Instead, it passes through the body and, as it does so, performs its magic. Some fiber helps reduce blood cholesterol, especially LDL ("bad" cholesterol) levels. Other fiber cleans the digestive tract and keeps it operating efficiently and effectively.

All fiber comes from plants and is either soluble or insoluble. Both kinds occur naturally in a wide array of foods and both are important. Soluble fiber, the kind that can absorb water and form gels, includes pectin, gums (such as guar gum), and mucilages. Insoluble fibers include cellulose and hemicellulose and lignin. The outer layers of food—skins, peels, husks—contain insoluble fiber. However, different parts of the plant may contain both soluble and insoluble fiber.

Good sources of soluble fiber include oat and rice brans, corn, apples, and citrus fruits. Good sources of insoluble fiber include legumes such as kidney and navy beans, strawberries and blackberries, pears, carrots, potatoes, and, last but not least, whole-grain breads.

THE HEALTH BENEFITS OF FIBER

The health benefits of a high-fiber diet are staggering. Once you understand them you will be as amazed as I am that back in the 1950s and 1960s the medical establishment believed fiber to be unimportant. Thankfully, nutrition researchers did not agree with such thinking and by the 1970s even the medical establishment was taking fiber seriously. Today, no one disputes its value.

When you consume a high fiber/high complex carbohydrate diet you will suffer less often from constipation, you will find it easier to lose and maintain weight, your blood cholesterol will lower, and you will most likely feel more alert during the day and sleep like a baby at night.

Evidence points to other benefits, too. With a high-fiber diet you are less likely to suffer from hemorrhoids, from irritable bowel syndrome, from diverticulosis and, perhaps, from ulcers. It may help prevent gall-stones, varicose veins, and the chance of appendicitis and Crohn's disease. Because it can lower blood cholesterol, it helps prevent atherosclerosis, the primary symptom of cardiovascular diseases, and it keeps blood sugars in good balance. Some studies support theories that a high-fiber/high complex carbohydrate, low-fat diet helps prevent colon, prostate, rectal, intestinal, and breast cancers. New research may link it to prevention of other cancers, too. A diet high in fiber and complex carbohydrates is routinely prescribed for diabetics, and sometimes does so much to keep blood sugars in check that they can, on the advice of their physician, give up insulin injections.

Anyone suffering from diabetes, heart disease, or any other ailment should consult his doctor before drastically changing his diet. Healthy people who are not getting their recommended share of complex carbohydrates and fiber should change their diet gradually but definitely.

HOW TO CHANGE YOUR DIET

I was raised on a nutritious diet that incorporated natural foods, many of which we grew ourselves. I rarely ate processed food. Every day my mother put whole-grain breads on the table along with fresh vegetables and fruits. Today, my wife, Christy, and I feed our four boys as I was fed growing up, all of us eating a vegetarian diet with an eye for the most natural, least processed foods we can grow, prepare, or buy.

I am not suggesting that you become a vegetarian. I am simply suggesting that you modify your diet to include more healthful foods that are high in vitamins, minerals, and fiber. Heed the advice of the experts: Plan on five or six servings of whole grains and legumes and four or five of fruits and vegetables every day. This ensures you are getting enough complex carbohydrates in your diet. Cut back on meat and whole dairy products, and try not to eat foods that include refined sugar or are high in sodium. Have a slice of bread rather than a doughnut and try one of my sweet breads instead of a rich, gooey dessert.

Take care to alter your diet gradually. If you are unused to high-fiber foods, add them to your diet in small amounts at first. As the weeks progress, add more and more fiber to acclimate your body gently. Before long, your system will welcome the increased amount of fiber. Be sure to eat lots of fruits and vegetables, too, to ensure that you get a full complement of vitamins and minerals and extra fiber.

If you are a vegetarian or want to try being one, there are numerous ways to ensure you get enough protein and calcium in the diet without eating animal foods. Eat plenty of legumes and green leafy vegetables, and (need I add?) eat thick, delicious slices of whole-grain breads.

Vegetarian or not, a bread machine is a valuble tool in the healthful kitchen. In a matter of minutes you can begin the process that, with no fuss or bother, results in freshly baked, whole-grain breads in about three hours.

WHOLE-GRAIN BREADS
FOR LOSING WEIGHT

It's true. I am not crazy. You can and *will* lose weight if you begin including healthful whole-grain breads in your diet. Remember, it is not the complex carbohydrate that puts on the pounds. It is the fat that often accompanies the carbohydrate: butter on toast, for instance, sour cream on baked potatoes, the butter or margarine in pound cakes, and the eggs in egg breads.

The breads I prefer are made without animal fats, without eggs, and without refined white sugar. They taste so good you will not want to smear them with sweetened jams and jellies. Eat them alone, with a little honey, or use them as sandwich bread for vegetarian fillings. For those of you with a sweet tooth, I have duplicated my mother's famous Honey-Cinnamon Rolls on page 96. Even a weight-watcher may indulge in these marvelously sweet and sticky creations once in a while.

Experts agree that our intake of complex carbohydrates should account for well over 50 percent of our total daily food. This is great news! Rice, pasta, breads, potatoes—all the foods you may have thought added pounds—are instead the ones you should eat. Season them with herbs, garlic, lemon juice, vinegar, tofu, lightly sautéed vegetables, or dried fruits. Decrease the amount of butter, cheese, oil, yogurt, and sour cream you use. If you eat dairy products, make sure to choose non-fat products such as skim milk and non-fat yogurt. Or, try small amounts of raw dairy products from the natural food store. Supplement these foods with lots of fresh vegetables and fruits, juices, and pure spring water. I guarantee: You will never feel deprived of good food and within a very short time you will notice the pounds melting away.

Nearly universally, people who reject a high-fat, protein-heavy diet and replace it with a high fiber/high carbohydrate one lose weight, feel better, and are able to maintain their weight without any trouble. This style of eating does away completely with the concept of "dieting." Instead, we are eating healthfully and well, enjoying every mouthful without feeling the pitiful deprivation "traditional" diets foist on us. We do not diet to reach a weight goal and then resume our old, slothful ways. No! We keep eating the high fiber/high carbohydrate foods, enjoying all the good flavors and wonderful dishes.

When you are concerned about your weight, remember my 70/30 rule. Eat healthfully nearly all the time, but the rest of the time keep in mind that life is a constant balancing act and you cannot chastise yourself for indulging in "bad" foods every now and again. Simply try to keep it to a minimum.

It is also important to exercise when trying to lose weight and when trying to maintain weight. I suggest walking briskly for several miles, or if you are up to it, bicycling, swimming, or aerobic dancing. Do whatever you enjoy: Play basketball, volleyball, or softball. Go skiing or take up horseback riding. Excess calories from carbohydrates burn off quickly—much faster than those from fat—and exercise will help them do so all the sooner. Exercise is important for cardiovascular health, and you will feel so much better when you are in good shape and have shed those few extra pounds.

CHAPTER ·3·

FLOUR AND GRAINS

A basic loaf of bread is a mixture of flour and water, raised by yeast or another leavener. While there are numerous variations on this theme, the essential formula changes little from recipe to recipe. Because I want you to appreciate the wonders of bread baking, I think it's important to define flour and to explain what constitutes a leavener. Both are simple ingredients and, with a little knowledge, any lingering fears you may have about making bread in your own kitchen will disappear like morning dew in the sunshine.

In this chapter I describe flour and the grains that make it. In Chapter 4 on page 32, I explain yeast and its considerable powers. Yeast is the king of leaveners, those agents that give bread its height and pleasingly spongy texture. But let's begin with flour.

I rely almost solely on flours made from whole grains. Whole wheat, with its good supply of gluten, is the most versatile, but I also bake breads that include flours made from grains such as amaranth, corn, millet, quinoa, oats, and rye. For anyone with a wheat gluten intolerance, I have provided a spelt bread recipe.

WHAT IS FLOUR?

Flour is the powdery substance that is the result of grinding grains (and sometimes seeds) in a mill. It is a starchy product that, because of its molecular makeup, has thickening abilities. In fact, the word starch derives from a German root meaning "stiff." Starches are glucose chains linked together to form polymers in which plants store excess energy.

Modern technology has produced giant mills that daily process tons of wheat and other grains to supply the nation's commercial and home bakers with flour. In ancient times, bakers ground grain between stones to make a crude flour that was baked into rough, sustaining loaves. Between the two milling extremes, flour has gone through many types of grinding, but all have sought the same objective: to turn hard seeds of grain into soft, powdery flour.

THE COMPOSITION OF GRAIN

All grains are composed of three parts: the bran, the endosperm, and the germ (or embryo). The bran is the tough, fibrous outer layer remaining after the grain is hulled. The endosperm, which comprises the bulk of the grain, is the starchy, protein-rich portion beneath the bran, and the germ is the center of the grain. The endosperm contains a protein called gluten. The germ is the most healthful part of the grain, with the most essential oils, vitamins, and minerals.

Gluten

While all grains—wheat, rye, quinoa, and so on—have brans, endosperms, and germs, not all contain gluten. Gluten is most evident in wheat, which explains why flours milled from wheat are the most versatile and most common for bread making.

When flour is mixed with liquid and then is warmed by kneading and baking, the gluten expands to form elastic strands capable of trapping bubbles of gas released by the yeast (see Chapter 4, page 34). The captured gas nestles in the gluten and raises the bread. Without gluten, the bread would be flat and dense.

Whole-Grain Flour

While all flour is made from grain, not all is made from the *whole* grain. All-purpose white flour is the endosperm alone; the bran and germ are removed. The end product is an excellent source of gluten, but it is *not* whole-grain flour. A good example of whole-grain flour is whole wheat flour, which contains the bran, endosperm, and germ. Flours made from grains such as rye and corn are always whole-grain flours and are categorically more nutritious than all-purpose white flour. Keep in mind that the best whole-grain flour with enough gluten to form a sturdy loaf is whole wheat flour. Other flours—rye, amaranth, etc.—are always combined with wheat flour for bread baking. It's also important to note that not all wheat flour is whole wheat flour. Flours labeled as wheat flour are generally white flour.

All-Purpose White Flour

Why, you ask, do we use white flour at all if whole-grain flour is clearly so much more nutritious? I try not to bake too often with white flour. The crinkly paper bags of all-purpose bleached flour lined up like plump soldiers on supermarket shelves have little place in my kitchen. However, I have discovered after much experimentation that white flour gives a lift and tenderness to some breads that cannot be achieved with whole-grain flour alone.

Universally, white flour is made from wheat because of its high gluten content and versatility. You will find white flour *and* whole-grain flour in the recipes I group under the subheading "transition breads"— breads designed to wean the home baker gradually and painlessly away from white flour and introduce him or her to the goodness of whole-grain flours.

I buy unbleached all-purpose white flour, never bleached flour. Whole wheat flour contains *as much* gluten as white flour, but because it is weighted down by the bran and germ, it generally does not produce as light a loaf as those made with white flour alone. But I believe it makes a far more healthful, better-tasting loaf.

Most flour looks white or off-white and is so finely ground that it resembles powder. This is true of both whole-grain and all-purpose flours. Every home baker knows that it is near impossible to bake without getting a residue of flour on the countertop and floor. Both the equipment and the employees at commercial bakeries are dusted with the white stuff, regardless of the diligence of the clean-up crew.

BUYING AND STORING FLOUR

Flour is sold in paper sacks in all supermarkets and groceries. Most home bakers buy it in five- or ten-pound quantities, although at some specialty and health food stores varieties are sold in bulk and you can scoop up as much as you like.

In general, buy flour as you need it. Store it in a cool, dry cupboard unopened in its packaging and once opened, transfer it to a glass or ceramic canister or jar with a tight-fitting lid. Most whole-grain flours keep for several months in a cool, dry place and for longer refrigerated. All-purpose white flour, bleached or unbleached, will keep for four or five months in a cool, dry cupboard and for longer in the refrigerator. Refrigeration makes the flour moister than when stored at room temperature. Hot, humid days also result in flours with higher moisture content, as does how the flour was milled, packaged, and shipped—all circumstances out of your control. In moist, warm climates and during the summer, it is hard to keep bugs out of the flour unless it is carefully stored. Remember to let flour that has been refrigerated come to room temperature before using it in the bread machine.

Storing Flour in the Freezer

The freezer is useful for storing whole-grain flours as it keeps them fresh far longer than the refrigerator. Wrap the unopened package in plastic, date it, and put it near the back of the compartment where it is coldest. Keep the flour frozen for up to four months. Let it come to room temperature before using it. Keep in mind that flour stored in the freezer will absorb moisture, just as it does in the refrigerator, and so the amount of flour called for in the recipe may have to be adjusted up slightly for the amount of liquid.

MILLING FLOUR

Milling grain into flour is an age-old process that has permitted mankind to take enormous advantage of the earth's cereal grains. Since grains are, by definition, small, hard seeds, their benefit to our diets is severely limited if they remain in their natural, whole state. Cooking and eating small, hard seeds is not easy. But when the seed is ground into a flour that readily combines with liquid and leavener and then can be baked into a glorious loaf of bread—that's sensible progress.

The tough fibrous bran protects the embryo (also called the germ) and the starchy endosperm. When white flour is the goal, the bran and germ are removed during milling so that what is left is the endosperm processed to a fine, white powder. When whole-grain flour is the goal, the bran and germ are ground with the endosperm. Because the bran and the germ contain nearly all the fiber, oil, and vitamins found in grains, as well as as much as a third of the protein, the whole-grain flour is far more healthful than white flour made from the endosperm alone. I realize I have already said this several times, but I cannot repeat it enough: It is very important.

For large food companies, the reasons for marketing white flour are far more compelling than my reasons for occasionally using it. Without the oil from the germ, which can spoil and turn rancid, the flour has a long shelf life. Its gluten protein renders it good for baking high-rising breads, and when unleavened (not mixed with yeast), the same flour produces tender cakes, crisp cookies, and flaky pastries not always possible with coarser, whole-grain wheat flour. White flour is, for the most part, uniform all across the nation. When you buy a five-pound sack of all-purpose white flour in Rhode Island you can be pretty sure it will react similarly to the five-pound sack of all-purpose you bought in Iowa or California. There are exceptions, depending on the part of the country you are in, but all in all, major food companies sell bleached, all-purpose flour to consumers who have been conditioned to tread a narrow path when it comes to home baking.

I believe such consistency is unnecessary—and no fun at all. What is more, during milling, giant rollers used by huge commercial mills generate high temperatures that effectively destroy the few nutrients that are present in the endosperm. The milled flour is treated with chlorine dioxide and benzyl peroxide to age and bleach it, and then is fortified with thiamin, riboflavin, niacin, and iron to compensate for the many nutrients lost during milling. Even flour labeled unbleached is often treated with acetone peroxide and azo-dicarbonimide. Hard-wheat bread flour may be bromated with potassium bromate to strengthen the flour's gluten. It is interesting to note that in California bromated flour is banned because it is a suspected carcinogen.

Stone-Ground Flours

In the old days, all flour was stone ground between large, grooved stones, one stationary and the other slowly rotated by a waterwheel. For this reason mills were built on rivers, and farm wagons from the surrounding area trundled to the mill with sheaves of harvested grain for grinding. Mind you, what came home from the mills was often coarse and mixed with harmless debris such as pebbles and straw from the primitive facility, but once the flour was sieved and cleaned, the fragrant breads that came from farm kitchens' ovens was undoubtedly beyond compare.

Today, small mills are springing up from coast to coast to grind flour the "old-fashioned" way. No longer do local farmers bring their own wheat for milling, but the mill buys grain—often organically raised grain—to grind and package under their own or a cooperative's label. You will find no stray bits of straw in this flour, but you will notice a difference in your bread. True, the millstones rarely are moved by waterwheels; electricity has taken over, but the flour is tended carefully. Most whole-grain stone-ground flours are not as fine as roller-ground flours and will yield a coarser, often heavier loaf with richer, earthier flavor.

Milling Grains at Home

It is no surprise that breads made from freshly ground flour are, to my mind, the best-tasting and the most nutritious. I buy whole grains from neighboring Montana ranchers and from reliable natural food stores. Once at home, I mill them in my own kitchen, using a small electric home mill and experimenting to my heart's content with different combinations of flour. I have planted a small field with wheat in back of my house this year and anxiously await the crop. I am looking forward to grinding the wheat berries from plants I sowed, nurtured, and harvested myself. A note of caution: Flour ground in hand-operated home mills tends to be heavy and is far better suited for breads made by hand. If you use it in the automatic bread maker, it could overburden the motor and cause the machine to stall. I have included an explanation of it, however, because I urge anyone interested in bread baking in general to try it at some time. Although not too many home bakers consider milling their own flour a convenient alternative to buying wholesome whole-grain flour, once you try it, you will discover that, like making your own pasta, it is a pleasurable experiment that is surprisingly simple. I promise, the flavor of the bread will be noticeably different: fuller, richer, tasting magnificently of the grain.

Neither food processors nor blenders are good choices for home grinding. If powerful enough, they may render the wheat berries to a powdery substance; for the correct consistency and the amount of flour necessary for even one loaf, you should purchase a home mill. These may be hand-cranked or electric. Some are fitted with granite stones and others with steel plates. Nearly all can be adjusted to control the fineness of the grind. Some electric mills will grind a variety of grains, even hard corn.

Hand-operated mills are far less expensive than electric mills, which often cost hundreds of dollars. Few home mills are sold in stores but instead have to be ordered through catalogs. Talk with the proprietor of your local health food store, or the baker who owns the best bread shop in town to learn more about them. There also are books, usually available in health food stores and well-stocked bookstores, that rate the machines. As with many appliances, price generally indicates power and quality. If you want to experiment and grind your own flour only now and then, a hand-cranked mill may be just fine; remember that it takes a laborious twenty minutes to grind enough wheat for a loaf of bread. If you are dedicated to making breads only with flour you grind yourself, investigate buying a more powerful machine or consider the idea of co-owning an electric one with a fellow bread baker.

A LIST OF GRAINS

Bread baking books include recipes that depend almost exclusively on wheat flour. This is for good reason: Wheat flour contains the most gluten, which is necessary for leavening. You can combine wheat flour with other flours, as I do throughout the book, to make all different sorts of bread.

This book is no different from any other in this regard, but with noted exceptions, I use only whole-grain flours, mixing whole-grain rye or buckwheat flour, for example, with whole wheat flour to ensure a full complement of gluten. I only use all-purpose unbleached white flour in the ''transition'' recipes, designed to help you get used to the idea of baking with whole-grain flours.

HEALTH BENEFITS OF GRAINS AND LEGUMES

Whole grains and legumes are recommended by the USDA and nutritionists as the foundation for a healthful diet. All grains and legumes are high in fiber, protein, and complex carbohydrates, and contain B-complex vitamins, calcium, chromium, magnesium, manganese, potassium, selenium, phosphorus, and zinc. All grains are also low in fat. This chart highlights some of the outstanding healthful qualities of many of the whole grains and legumes called for in my recipes.

GRAIN OR LEGUME	VITAMINS & MINERALS	HELPFUL FOR; SPECIAL CONSIDERATIONS	SAMPLE RECIPE
Amaranth	Protein, lysine, vitamin C, beta carotene, calcium, iron, potassium	Protein requirements; cardiovascular system & digestive tract	Amaranth Soy Bread (see page 88)
Barley	Protein, niacin, folic acid, thiamin, calcium, magnesium, phosphorus	Helps lower cholesterol; 2.2 grams fat per cup	Sesame Barley Bread (see page 156)
Buckwheat	Bioflavonoid rutin, protein, thiamin, folic acid, vitamin B6, calcium, iron	Helps strengthen capillaries, may help prevent strokes; 2.6 grams fat per cup	Buckwheat Oat Bread (see page 82)
Corn	Protein, lysine, vitamin A, folic acid, potassium, calcium, phosphorus, potassium	Contains anti-cancer agents; 3 grams fat per cup	Cornmeal Herb Bread (see page 180)
Kamut	Protein, pantothenic acid, calcium, magnesium, phosphorus, potassium	Usually well tolerated by wheat-sensitive people	Kamut Bread (see page 70)

	Nutrients	Description	Bread
Millet	Protein, calcium, iron, magnesium, potassium, phosphorus	The only grain that is alkaline when cooked; most complete protein	High-Protein Bread (see page 86)
Oats	Protein, calcium, potassium, vitamin A, thiamin, pantothenic acid	Helps lower cholesterol; high in anti-oxidants, which prevents rancidity	Oat Bran Bread (see page 72)
Potato	Protein, iron, vitamin C, potassium, phosphorus	Gluten-free; very low fat	Wholesome Potato Bread (see page 136)
Quinoa	Protein, calcium, iron, phosphorus, vitamin E, lysine	Helps strength and endurance; high calcium: 1 cup = 1 qt. milk	Quinoa and Sesame Seed Bread (see page 84)
Rye	Calcium, magnesium, lysine, potassium	Low gluten; helps immune system and bone growth	Caraway Onion Bread (see page 178)
Soybean	Protein, calcium, vitamin A, vitamin B6, lecithin, iron, phosphorus, folic acid, copper, magnesium	Helps prevent cirrhosis of the liver; 17.6 grams fat per cup	High-Protein Bread (see page 86)
Spelt	Protein, riboflavin, niacin, thiamin, iron, potassium	Contains gluten, but is usually tolerated by wheat-sensitive people	Spelt Bread (see page 92)
Wheat	Protein, calcium, iron, magnesium, phosphorus, potassium, B-complex vitamins	Strong gluten capabilities; multipurpose flour; reacts well with yeast, and combines well with all other grains	100 Percent Whole Wheat Bread (see page 66)

The flours I call for in the recipes may be unfamiliar to you, but after a trip to a large natural food store and after reading the following descriptions of each one, they will cease to be exotic and mysterious. After all, they are, for the most part, cereal grains ground into flour. Nothing more, nothing less. And for a quick review of their healthful properties, see the chart on pages 22–23.

The following list is arranged alphabetically. Within the text of each entry I explain any special storing requirements. Get to know the flours and learn their many possibilities. Bread baking, even with an easy-to-use, top-quality bread machine, is not an exact science. But the results are always delicious.

Please note that I have included bean flours and flaxseed on this list. They do not fall under the category of "grains," but because I use them as flours, I define them here.

Amaranth: This specialty flour is becoming increasingly available although it is still most often found in natural food stores. The coarse, beige-colored flour is ground from tiny seeds that are high in protein, calcium, iron, and phosphorus. It is practically gluten-free, however, and must be combined with wheat flour. Use amaranth in small amounts—about one part amaranth flour to three or four parts wheat flour—for nutritious loaves with nutty, earthy flavor. Amaranth flour is also good in pancakes and muffins when mixed with milder wheat flour. Buy it in small packages.

Barley: Barley is the fourth most widely grown grain in the world. Barley flour is used most frequently in Asia for bread baking, although the low-fat flour is attracting bread bakers in this country as well who combine it with wheat flour in proportions up to one part barley to four parts wheat. Store barley flour as you would any whole-grain flour.

Buckwheat: Perhaps pancakes come to mind when you think of buckwheat and, indeed, the flour makes tasty flapjacks. Buckwheat is not a cereal grain; its seeds come from a plant related to rhubarb and sorrel that grows best in cold climates and is frequently found in Russian and Middle European cooking. In the U.S., we sometimes call buckwheat *kasha* and often eat buckwheat groats, which are minimally processed buckwheat seeds.

Buckwheat flour looks gray-brown and if stone ground is flecked with dark specks of the hull. The flour contains little gluten but is high in protein and fiber. Its discernible grassy flavor makes it a likely candidate for mixing with blander wheat or a combination of wheat and other flours. Buckwheat flour is available in natural food stores as well as many supermarkets.

Corn: Corn flour is more finely ground than cornmeal and both are derived from dent or flint corn—not sweet corn, although baked goods made with corn flour taste noticeably sweet. The best corn flour is stone ground from the whole kernel. Corn flour and cornmeal usually are noticeably yellow, reflecting their grain of origin. Some, made from white corn, are cream-colored. Neither has much gluten and recipes including one or the other often are raised by the addition of eggs and/or chemical leaveners such as baking powder and baking soda. I combine corn flour and cornmeal with whole wheat flour and rely on the gluten in the latter to leaven loaves that, once baked, have crunchy, crumbly textures and pleasing sweet flavor.

Flaxseed: Flaxseed is not a cereal grain and few people think of using flaxseed or flaxseed flour for baking. However, I like to use it whenever I can, as it blends well with wheat flour and provides a good share of linolenic acid. Linolenic acid may help keep tumors from forming, and some studies show it helps protect against asthma, arthritis, and psoriasis. Flaxseed is available in natural food stores. Store flaxseed and flaxseed flour in a cool, dark place.

Garbanzo beans: Flours made by grinding beans are not true flours in that they do not derive from a seed containing a germ and endosperm. But they are nutritious in their own right (no one disputes the value of legumes in a healthful diet!) and when added in judicious amounts to bread dough, they provide vitamins, minerals, and protein. Although we don't have any recipes that use garbanzo flour you can try substituting ½ cup for any other flour in your favorite bread.

Gluten flour: As the name suggests, this product is mainly gluten, the protein that reacts with yeast and gives bread its lovely rise. It also may be called vital wheat gluten or high gluten flour. Like all-purpose white flour, gluten flour is made from the endosperm of wheat, but the process is taken several steps further. The starch is removed and the remaining gluten is ground again and then combined with very finely milled white flour (called patent flour) for a product that is about 50 percent gluten.

Gluten flour is never used in much quantity; I add it to most of the whole-grain bread doughs (elite recipes) to give them an extra lift. You can buy it in natural food stores. Buy small amounts and store it in a cool, dry place. It keeps well for several months.

Kamut: A new form of an ancient grain, Kamut was cultivated in Egypt during the time of the pharoahs, and today is grown in Montana. Compared to other strains of wheat, Kamut production is small but the popularity of the grain is growing, particularly among vegetarians and people on macrobiotic diets. Kamut kernels are more than twice the size of other wheat kernels and its protein levels are high: 15 to 18 percent compared with 12 or 16 percent in hard wheat. Nevertheless, its gluten content is low and it almost always is used in tandem with whole wheat flour. One of the benefits of Kamut is that it tends to be less allergenic than other wheat flours. It has more calories, too, and higher concentrations of magnesium and zinc. Kamut berries sprout very easily and can be used in place of sprouted wheat berries. Store Kamut in a cool, dry place.

Millet: Millet is a grass with a tiny seed that flourishes even in poor soil and as such is an important global grain. It is used extensively throughout India and the rest of Asia and is gaining in popularity here. Millet meal or whole millet may be added to bread for crunch, moisture, and subtle but toasty flavor. Millet flour is a tremendous source of protein and I use it in some breads. Millet can be cooked like rice and served as a breakfast cereal. Store it in a cool, dark place.

Oats: Oats have traditionally been eaten in cold, damp climates, where they not only flourish but where they nourish a population in need of filling, robust food. The product that we think of as ''oatmeal'' is simply steel-cut oat groats (minimally processed grains) that have been flattened by huge rollers. These cook in minutes for a satisfying, thick porridge. Oats are good sources of vitamin E and thiamin and are high in carbohydrates. Oat bran is a good source of soluble dietary fiber, which means it helps lower blood cholesterol levels (see Chapter 2, page 11, for more on the benefits of fiber). Oats also have a little more fat than other grains, although no grains are high in fat or calories, and oats themselves represent about 130 calories per cooked cup. Use old-fashioned rolled oats in my recipes—not quick cooking or instant oatmeal.

Oat flour adds sweet flavor to wheat breads and because it is full of antioxidants, the grain has a longer shelf life than most others. When combined with whole wheat, the baked loaf stays fresh a little longer than usual. This same property makes oat flour, steel-cut groats, and oatmeal well suited for lengthy storage. Oat products keep about twice as long as other grain products when stored in a cool, dry place.

Potato flour: Potato flour is also called potato starch and is a weighty powder that adds moistness to some bread doughs. Potato starch is sometimes mixed with a powder made from kuzo, itself a starchy root that, like arrowroot, is used most often to thicken sauces. Some manufacturers call potato starch "kuzo," which is inaccurate. Check the ingredient list when buying potato starch or flour—and, conversely, when buying kuzo for other kitchen purposes. Potato starch, found in Kosher sections of the supermarket, stores well and will keep for several months in a cool place.

Quinoa: No doubt you have heard about this grain but may not be sure what it is or even how to pronounce it. Quinoa ("keen-wa") is a highly nutritious grain that originated centuries ago in South America and grows well at high altitudes and in rocky soil. With the arrival of the Spanish in the 1600s, cultivation of quinoa diminished as the European conqueror burned the grain fields. In recent years it has experienced a renaissance. It is therefore no surprise that quinoa is currently being raised in North America's Rocky Mountains and food watchers have high hopes for the growing popularity of the hardy plant.

For a grain, it is an excellent source of iron, phosphorus, calcium, vitamin E, and some B vitamins. Quinoa has a good balance of amino acids, particularly lysine, usually low in grains. It is higher in protein than any other grain, but not high in gluten and so must be combined with wheat flour for bread baking. Like all whole-grain flours, quinoa flour should be stored in a cool, dry place and used within a month or six weeks.

If you buy quinoa in its whole-grain form, be sure it has been cleaned to rid it of bitter-tasting saponin, a sticky covering that naturally repels birds and insects in the field. If you are not certain the grain is saponin-free, wash it in water and rinse and drain it well.

Rice: Plain and simple, rice feeds half the world, coming in a close second to wheat in global production. In the U.S. we tend to think only of processed white rice, which is milled so that the beige-colored and nutrient-rich outer layers of bran are removed. Brown rice tastes nuttier and fuller and is markedly better for you.

There are numerous kinds of rice—far too many to describe here—but basically rice is classified by grain size (long-grain, short-grain, etc.). Short-grain rices tend to be more sticky than long-grain rices and are used most often in sweets and in Asian dishes. Longer-grained rices are commonly found in savory pilafs, casseroles, and salads.

Rice flour is made from all sorts of rice, but the short-grain rices produce a product that is best used as a thickener. Flour milled from long-grain brown rice can be used in bread. Rice flour is available in many supermarkets, Asian markets, and natural food stores. Store it as you would any whole-grain flour.

Rye: Rye was one of the most popular flours in medieval times throughout northern Europe and the area we now call Russia. Even today most rye production is in Poland and Russia, where dark breads such as pumpernickel and black bread are important dietary staples. In the U.S., we think of rye bread only for sandwiches, yet combined with wheat flour, rye flour bakes into distinctive, bold-tasting, homey loaves with chewy crusts that are welcome at nearly any meal. Although there are three kinds of rye, light, medium, and dark, I like medium rye in my recipes. Pumpernickel rye is darker-colored flour.

Rye flour is high in the essential amino acid lysine. It has less protein than wheat and consequently poor gluten power; it must be combined with whole wheat flour to make a raised loaf, and even so should be treated with care as its natural starches cause it to swell a little more than other flours. Rye is often used in flatbreads, especially those favored by the Scandinavians. The coarse, dark-specked flour has very little taste raw but once baked, its full flavor emerges in all its glory and specks of the rye bran are plain to see in the baked loaf. Store it as you do other whole-grain flours, in a cool, dry place.

Soy beans: When added to wheat flour, yellow soy flour conditions the dough so that the loaves rise to loftier heights than normal, due to the work of active enzymes. However, too much soy flour in a recipe will give the bread an unpleasant flavor. Follow the recipes calling for soy flour carefully to avoid overusing it. Soy flour is sold in natural food stores, many supermarkets, and some Asian markets. Store soy flour in the refrigerator.

Spelt: You may never have heard of spelt, which is not surprising since the grain, ancient though its origins may be, is relatively new to twentieth-century agriculture. The grain can be used in place of wheat in some recipes. This is beneficial for anyone with a wheat allergy. Spelt, which is perhaps the easiest grain to digest, is also high in the B vitamins and minerals such as potassium and iron. Buy spelt in natural food stores and progressive supermarkets and store it in a cool, dark place.

Wheat: The Western diet is based on wheat consumption. It forms the basis for nearly all our breads as well as for numerous other foods such as breakfast cereals, crackers, and pasta. Americans eat far more wheat than any other grain—more than 75 percent of our grain consumption is wheat. Quite frankly, without wheat flour, bread baking would be a lost art. Its naturally high gluten content makes it by far the best flour for our purposes.

Wheat is classified by its time and place of planting. Hard spring wheat, planted in the spring in northern climes, has more gluten than hard winter wheat although both are considered good for breads. Soft wheat, grown in warmer areas, has less gluten and traditionally has been used for recipes that do not rely on gluten development, such as biscuits, cakes, and pastries.

All-purpose flours are a blending of wheat flours and tend to be uniform from region to region and state to state. They perform adequately for bread and cake baking both—but not superbly for either. As you no doubt know, I prefer whole wheat flour for bread. Its gluten development is excellent and it is highly nutritious and extremely versatile. When buying whole wheat flour, look for varieties with high-protein content listed on the side of the bag or box. Fourteen to 16 grams per cup of flour will afford the best results. Whole wheat pastry flour does not have enough protein to produce a sturdy loaf, so be sure not to purchase it by mistake.

Once you start making breads in the automatic bread machine, you no doubt will want to buy whole wheat flour in large quantities. It is sold in supermarkets, and the national brands are acceptable. But I like to mill my own or buy it in natural food stores where I can scoop as much as I need from a barrel and tote it home in a brown paper sack. Make sure your natural food store has good turnover of the flour. Store it as you do other whole-grain flours, in a cool, dry place or in the refrigerator.

THE ROLE OF YEAST
AS LEAVENER

A leavener is an ingredient that, due to its reactions to liquid and heat, causes a baked good to rise. Whether you are baking a cake, a soufflé, muffins, popovers, or bread, you rely on a leavener for the desired texture and height.

THE DIFFERENT LEAVENERS

There are several leaveners. The most common are baking powder and baking soda, which are called chemical leaveners; second are eggs and fats, which leaven by aerating the food; and third is yeast. Baking powder and baking soda work alone or together, depending on the alkaline-acid balance of the other ingredients in the recipe. These common household items raise familiar baked goods such as cakes, muffins, and quick breads. When mixed with liquid, they release carbon dioxide and the expanding gas leavens the baked good. Beaten egg whites, which incorporate a lot of air, leaven fragile soufflés. Egg-enforced batter expands and traps air to raise popovers and Yorkshire pudding. Both soufflés and popovers, leavened only by hot air, deflate easily and quickly once taken from the oven.

Yeast is the leavener preferred by the majority of bread bakers, and definitely is my first choice. For my breads, I buy yeast at natural food stores or the active dry yeast sold in supermarkets in foil-lined envelopes or sealed jars. Yeast varies from brand to brand. For the recipes in this book, I got the best rise with Red Star yeast. If the bread does not rise properly, be prepared to increase the amount of yeast by about one teaspoon for the one-and-a-half pound loaves, and half a teaspoon for the one-pound loaves.

The most important thing to remember about any yeast is that it must be "alive" to work. Therefore, check the date on the package and, if in doubt or the recipe calls for it, proof the yeast in warm liquid to test its capabilities. I will explain how to do this later in this chapter.

WHAT IS YEAST?

Yeast, a single-celled living microorganism, is probably the oldest leavener used by man. No one knows who discovered its abilities to raise a dough of flour and water to lofty heights, but no doubt the earliest yeasts were kept alive in what we call sourdough starter: a slurry of flour and water that attracts yeast spores from the air and, as it ferments, becomes a natural leavening agent. Sourdough starters are still popular with bakers who feed and nurture their own mother mixtures and commonly share them with other bread bakers. I discuss sourdough starters in more depth on page 35.

Active Dry Yeast

Today, we rely on active dry yeast, a granular powder sold most familiarly in premeasured packets, to leaven bread. When the tiny, one-celled yeast microorganisms come into contact with moisture and heat, they rapidly divide and multiply. This action takes place when the bread dough is being kneaded and again, most noticeably, as it rises and bakes.

Compressed Yeast and Rapid Rise Yeast

You may be tempted to buy cakes of compressed yeast, the sort used by our grandmothers. Compressed yeast cakes are not well suited for the bread machine and, therefore, not recommended. I always call for active dry yeast, a product perfected shortly after World War II and that in many respects revolutionized home bread baking.

I do not suggest rapid rise yeast for my recipes. The time-saving product works well for some recipes, but not for the recipes I have developed especially for the bread machine. Stay with the standard active dry yeast for the best results.

Proofing Yeast

When you use a bread machine, proofing is not necessary, but because it is integral to many traditional bread recipes, I will explain its purpose. Proofing is just what it says it is—a method for proving that the yeast is active and alive. To proof, sprinkle yeast over warm water and a tiny bit of honey or other sweetener: In a matter of minutes the solution begins to bubble and foam and before you know it is crowned with a swollen, frothy cap. When this happens, you can be sure the yeast is alive and well and will work beautifully in your bread. However, because active dry yeast is so reliable, there is no need to proof it for my recipes for the bread machine.

Proofing also gets the yeast off to a ''good start,'' or, in other words, initiates the cell division that makes it work. This is more important for hand-kneaded breads, where the conditions are not as ideal as the environment in the bread machine with its steady, rhythmical kneading action and warm, contained canister designed for perfect rising. When using the automatic bread maker, be sure to measure yeast accurately.

MEASURING, STORING, AND BUYING YEAST

I buy yeast in sealed packets and jars from natural food stores, where I can be sure it is fresh. Most home bakers rely on envelopes of Fleischmann's and Red Star active dry yeast available from Honolulu to Hoboken in the refrigerator sections of supermarkets and grocery stores. These packets contain approximately two and three-quarter teaspoons of yeast.

Keep all yeast in the refrigerator in tightly sealed containers; clean, glass baby food jars with screw-on lids are good choices for loose yeast. Because the temperature of the refrigerator is lower than 50 degrees Fahrenheit, the yeast will lie dormant for several months. It will *not* last any longer in the freezer. I do not suggest keeping yeast for longer than three months, whether it is stored in the refrigerator or the freezer.

When buying yeast in packets, check the "use before" or "good until" date. As with all dated products, the date most distant from the day of purchase is the best assurance of freshness. Both Fleischmann's and Red Star sell small jars of loose yeast granules, which also are dated. As with the packets, these should be stored in the refrigerator after opening.

If you buy yeast from a natural food store, be sure you buy bakers' yeast, not nutritional or brewers' yeast. These two products will not leaven bread. Often all three yeasts are displayed near each other and so it behooves you to be careful. Bakers' yeast is clearly marked and if it is not dated, do so when you get home to help keep track of its freshness.

HOW DOES YEAST WORK?

Yeast feeds on the sugar naturally produced by the starch in the flour as it is manipulated (kneaded) and combined with liquid. As the yeast cells grow and multiply, they release carbon dioxide and vaporized alcohol. These gases are trapped by gluten protein, which develops into elastic strands during kneading, which are capable of holding the minuscule balloonlike bubbles of gas in the dough. The gases give the bread height; the gluten gives it structure.

Yeast is dormant at temperatures lower than 50 degrees Fahrenheit. Heated to more than 120 degrees Fahrenheit, it dies. It multiplies best at temperatures between 80 and 110 degrees Fahrenheit. This is why we mix it with warm water for proofing when baking bread conventionally—the swelling that occurs not only tells us the yeast is alive, it gets the leavening process going. Many recipes call for a small amount of sugar in the proofing liquid as yeast feeds on sugar. I do not use refined sugar but rely instead on the converted starch from the flour and, at times, alternative sweeteners to feed the yeast in the warm environment of the bread machine.

The gluten continues to develop and the yeast to work during kneading, rising, and then, finally, during baking. The heat of the oven or bread machine is the last big push for the yeast-gluten activity. When the bread dough reaches a temperature hotter than 120 degrees, the yeast dies and the gases dissipate. The bread has risen to its highest point and from this juncture, the cellular structure sets and firms while the characteristic bread crust forms. If the bread has been improperly kneaded, it may taste "yeasty." If the bread is tough and dry, it is overbaked. Rarely do either of these problems have anything to do with the yeast—and both are rare when you use a bread machine with its foolproof, built-in kneading, resting, and baking cycles.

Yeast does work more effectively if it is used high above sea level. You will need to decrease the amount you use in the machine if you live in a high altitude part of the country. See page 53 for special instructions.

Using Yeast in the Bread Machine

For the bread machine, you do not proof the yeast. If the yeast is fresh, add it directly to the machine when called for. In my recipes this is at the end, after the flour is spooned over the liquid. To test a questionable envelope of yeast—one with a borderline date, for example—stir a pinch or so of it in lukewarm water along with ⅛ teaspoon of honey. If you use loose yeast, you may choose to proof ½ teaspoon of yeast in about a quarter cup of warm water with ¼ teaspoon of honey, and once satisfied of its viability—evidenced by noticeable swelling and foaming—discard the proofed sample. If you rely on packets, take no more than one sixteenth of a teaspoon and stir it into about a tablespoon of water with a drop of honey and watch for the reaction. This way, you will not upset the balance of yeast to flour if that is the only packet of yeast you have left to use for the bread.

The best way to ensure success is to buy yeast in relatively small quantities and use it within a few months. Discard old yeast and renew your supply regularly. If the baked loaves are deflated or low, it's a good bet the yeast you used was past its prime and should be replaced.

SOURDOUGH STARTERS

Sourdough starters are the most ancient forms of leavening yeast. Early civilizations discovered the leavening powers of fermented flour and water. No doubt they also recognized the fermenting properties of the starter's liquid run-off and used it to make vinegar and primitive wines.

Modern bread bakers usually have a batch of sourdough starter on the back shelf of the refrigerator or stowed in the freezer ready to make tender loaves with distinctive tangy flavor. But if you do not have a starter of your own, it is an easy matter to make one.

Starters can be acquired four different ways: You can grow your own from a mixture of flour, honey, and water; you can grow one from a little starter that you have borrowed; you can culture a starter from a mixture of active dry yeast, flour, water, and honey; or you can buy sourdough granules in a kit from a natural food store or specialty shop. I recommend the last two options, unless you have a friend with an exceptionally good, strong starter.

Making a Sourdough Starter

On pages 134 and 135 I have formulas for making starter from active dry yeast, using both *unbleached* white flour and whole wheat flour. If you decide to use a kit, follow the package directions. Once you have the starter going, keep it alive by adding equal measures of unbleached white flour or whole wheat flour and water to it every time you use it. Be sure to use the type of flour with which you originally began. If the starter seems inactive or develops a strong, sour odor, stir about four tablespoons of the starter into a cup of flour mixed with a cup of water and leave it at warm room temperature for several hours until it begins to bubble and expand. If the smell is distinctively ''off'' and the liquid looks pinkish, discard it and begin again. Clear liquid is acceptable; simply pour it off before measuring the starter.

Storing Sourdough Starters

Store sourdough starters in pottery crocks, glass jars, or porcelain tubs, loosely covered, in the refrigerator. Do not use metal; the starter will corrode it. Even if you do not use it, check the starter every week or ten days and refresh it with more flour and water, stirring it gently and letting it sit at warm room temperature until bubbling, about 30 minutes, before returning it to the refrigerator.

Warmth is vital to a sourdough starter. The yeast spores flourish at temperatures over 85 degrees Fahrenheit and the starter comes alive with bubbles and foam. But once the temperature tops 95 degrees Fahrenheit, the starter dies. On the other hand, cold will not hurt it and refrigeration keeps it dormant. If you know you will not use the starter for several weeks, freeze about a cup in a plastic bag or container. Let the frozen starter come to room temperature and then revitalize it with equal measures of flour and water.

Breads baked with sourdough starters taste wonderful and keep a little longer than other breads. Sourdough starters will raise the bread as high as any yeast does although the rising must take place in a particularly warm area (about 85°) for the starter to work. This is no problem with the bread machine, which has a moist, warm environment that ensures an even, slow, and steady rise.

THE INDISPUTABLE
BENEFITS OF
A BREAD MACHINE

Although I could provide a dozen reasons why you will love using a bread machine, I have come up with four that I think will convince you right away. First, the machine is a great time saver; second, the bread it produces is consistently excellent; third, the machine is energy and cost efficient; and fourth, it requires practically no clean up.

As I say in Chapter 7, I think making bread by hand is a wonderful exercise and one that everyone should experience, but realistically, rarely do many of us have the time to make bread this way. When the automatic bread maker becomes part of your kitchen, the problem of time disappears and you are able to bake fresh bread every single day. Never again will you have to eat three- or four-day old bread, and the just-baked, whole-grain bread is especially nutritious.

When you bake bread following my recipes for the appropriate-sized machine, the finished loaf comes from the baking canister beautifully browned and nicely rounded time after time. Such consistency is worth a lot to the home baker. The machine minimizes guesswork. You never have to wonder if you over- or under-kneaded, let the bread rise too much or not enough, baked it for the right amount of time or overbaked it. The machine does it all.

If you have baked bread in a conventional oven during the height of the summer, you know how hot the kitchen gets. No one likes spending time in the sweltering room, least of all you! With the bread machine, you don't have to worry about preheating the oven, checking the bread for doneness, or letting the large oven cool down. The self-contained bread machine kneads, rests, rises, *and* bakes the bread—and then turns itself off. The mini-oven hardly heats the kitchen up at all, although the heavenly aroma of baking bread wafts through the house just the same. What is more, the bread machine requires only 120 volts of power, while most electric ovens need 240 volts. Without preheating time and with its automatic shut-off, the bread machine will hardly affect your electric bill.

Finally, I can, if necessary, bake bread wearing a suit and tie. I admit, this is not my preferred costume for baking (or almost anything else!), but when I am running off to a meeting or to church, my garb does not prevent me from combining the liquid, flour, and yeast in the baking canister, closing the lid, and pushing the button. No mess, no fuss. Best of all, when I get home, the bread is ready—and no mixing bowls or greasy bread pans are waiting in the kitchen sink. The baking canister needs only a quick rinse and toweling-off before it is stowed in the machine for the next time.

HOW THE BREAD MACHINE WORKS

The concept is so simple you may find yourself wondering why no one thought of it earlier. An automatic bread machine duplicates the four essential steps required for bread baking: mixing, kneading, rising, and baking. All four are performed in the same container, and not one requires your time. You can also dispense with the baking cycle, if you so desire, and remove the risen dough to make free-form loaves and rolls.

The handsome, boxy bread machine sits on the countertop. Under the lid is a rectangular bread canister, or bread pan, equipped with a handle for easy lifting. A kneading drive shaft protrudes through the bottom of the bread canister, onto which is fitted a removable kneading blade. When the ingredients for the bread are placed in the canister and the machine is activated, the kneading blade first stirs the ingredients and then, once they have formed into a dough ball, kneads the dough for a programmed period of time. After the dough is kneaded, it rises inside the gently warmed bread canister. If you peek through the viewing window (you are advised not to open the lid) at the end of the rising time, you will see that the soft dough has expanded to the corners of the pan and risen nearly to the rim of the bread pan. At this point the bread machine automatically raises its internal temperature to about

300° (depending on the cycle) and the bread bakes. When done, the machine beeps, signaling that the job is complete. Take care not to block the air vents during baking; steam may rise from these vents during baking, a perfectly normal occurrence. The box on page 46 describes the different settings and their lengths of time for the Breadman Bread Machine.

It is also possible to delay the entire process conveniently by using the timer built into the bread machine. This means you can put the necessary ingredients into the canister early in the morning and set the timer so that the bread is finished shortly after you get home from work at the end of the afternoon. Or set it at night so that a warm breakfast greets you when you wake up. Both features render the machine wonderfully versatile.

Most electric bread machines make either one- or one-and-a-half-pound loaves and both yield generous slices, perfect for hearty sandwiches bursting with the goodness of whole grains. My recipes are developed for both sizes of loaf, depending on your needs. The Breadman is a one-and-a-half-pound-capacity machine that can also make a one-pound loaf. Some manufacturers sell machines with a one-pound capacity only. Be sure you know the capacity of your machine and use the appropriate recipe; otherwise you may be courting failure. How do you tell? If a recipe calls for 3 cups of flour, it's a 1½-pound loaf. Two cups of flour is a 1-pound loaf.

ALL BREAD MACHINES ARE DIFFERENT

While my recipes work perfectly in the Breadman and most other automatic bread makers, they may need a little adjustment for some bread machines. Turn to the chart on pages 42–44 for this information. Essentially, all bread machines employ the same principles: The ingredients are combined in a single canister, mixed and kneaded mechanically, and then baked inside the machine.

For many machines, including mine, the liquid ingredients are put in the canister first, followed by the dry ingredients and then the yeast. Instructions for other machines may ask that you put the yeast in first, then the dry ingredients and finally the liquids. In either case, the liquid and the yeast are kept separate until mixing begins to prevent the yeast from activating before it should. Because of this, some electric bread machines are made with a special yeast dispenser.

Different bread machines have different settings on the display panel.

ADJUSTMENTS FOR USING DIFFERENT BREAD MACHINES AND SETTING/CYCLE EQUIVALENTS

BREAD MACHINE	BASIC WHEAT SETTING*	EUROPEAN SETTING	FRUIT & NUT SETTING	DOUGH SETTING	SPECIAL ADJUSTMENTS, IF ANY
Breadman 1 & 1½ pounds	Basic Wheat setting*	European setting	Fruit & Nut setting	Dough setting	None
Chefmate HB-12W	Standard setting	French Bread setting	Sweet setting	Dough setting	None
Dak	White Bread setting	French Bread setting	Sweet setting	Manual setting	For all recipes, add 2 tablespoons (1 ounce) water & ½ teaspoon yeast
Hitachi HB-8101/8201 1½ pounds	Bread setting	Bread setting	Mix Bread setting	Dough setting	For all recipes, add ½ teaspoon yeast
Magic Mill Auto Bakery 101 1½ pounds	White Bread setting	French Bread setting	Sweet setting	Manual setting	For all recipes, add 2 tablespoons (1 ounce) water & ½ teaspoon yeast
300 1 pound	Auto setting	Auto setting	Auto setting	Manual setting	None

	Standard setting	French Bread setting	Rye Bread setting	Dough setting	
Maxim Accu-Bakery BB-1 1 pound	Standard setting	French Bread setting	Rye Bread setting	Dough setting	None
MK Seiko Home Bakery					
HB-12W 1 pound	Standard setting	French Bread setting	Sweet setting	Dough setting	None
Mister Loaf HB-210/215 1½ pounds	Standard setting	French Bread setting	Sweet setting	Dough setting	None
National/ Panasonic					
SD-B155P 1 pound	Basic Bake setting	Basic Bake setting	Basic Bake setting	Dough setting	None
SD-B165N 1½ pounds	Basic Bake setting	Crisp setting	Basic Bake setting	Dough setting	For all recipes, decrease yeast by ½ teaspoon and add 2 tablespoons (1 ounce) water
Regal K6772	Bread setting	Bread setting	Raisin Bread setting	Dough setting	None
Sanyo	Bread setting	Bread setting	Bread setting	Dough setting	None

BREAD MACHINE	BASIC WHEAT SETTING*	EUROPEAN SETTING	FRUIT & NUT SETTING	DOUGH SETTING	SPECIAL ADJUSTMENTS, IF ANY
Welbilt					
ABM-100 1½ pounds	White Bread setting	French Bread setting	Sweet setting	Manual setting	For all recipes, add 2 tablespoons water (1 ounce) and ½ teaspoon yeast
ABM 300/350/ 600 1 pound	Auto setting	Auto setting	Auto setting	Manual setting	None
Zojirushi BBCC-S15 1½ pounds	Basic White setting	French Bread setting	Raisin Bread setting	Dough setting	For all recipes, add 2 tablespoons (1 ounce) water and ½ teaspoon yeast

*There are three Basic Wheat settings for the Breadman machine—Light, Medium, and Dark. If the recipe says Basic Wheat cycle, Light, Medium, or Dark setting, choose the setting for your machine that corresponds to the Basic Wheat setting on this chart.

Most are equipped with a setting for "normal" breads, for wheat breads, for dark-crusted breads, for European (or French) breads, for sweet (or raisin) breads, and for dough alone. The Breadman bread machine, which I helped design, has special cycle settings. The Fruit & Nut setting is designed for those sweet bread recipes calling for raisins, nuts, dates, and other weighty ingredients that make the dough heavy and require the machine to work a little harder than usual. The Breadman machine is specially equipped to mix and knead robust whole-grain flours, a feature I particularly appreciate and that is clearly indicated on the control panel. The Breadman provides a Basic Wheat setting with three options: light, medium, and dark. The recipes direct you to the appropriate setting. The chart on pages 42–44 explains the various settings on most of the other electric bread machines on the market. The chart also explains how to adjust the recipes for the different machines, and the tips beginning on page 50 in Chapter 6 will answer other questions you have.

Depending on the setting required for a recipe, the Breadman can take from 2 hours and 20 minutes to 3 hours and 40 minutes to bake a loaf of bread. To help you get to know the machine before you use it, I have listed here the times of the various cycles. These times apply only to the Breadman, although other machines may have similarly timed cycles.

When you purchase a bread machine, read the manual carefully. Operating instructions are similar but far from identical, and no two machines perform exactly alike. I believe my machine produces the most tasty breads with the best, most pleasing textures. It is fitted with a 1.5-meter-long power cord, which means it can be plugged in at a convenient distance from the nearest socket. The timer spans two-and-a-half hours to twelve hours. If the thermal temperature of the baking cavity reaches 370° Fahrenheit the Breadman automatically turns off—whether the bread is done or not! This safety feature is designed to make you feel secure about leaving the appliance plugged in when you are away from the house.

CARING FOR THE BREAD MACHINE

Because there is only one moving part in the bread machine, care and maintenance are simple. The kneading blade rotates on its shaft and is easily removed for cleaning with a damp sponge or cloth. If it sticks, pour a little warm water into the bread case to help loosen it. Use wooden toothpicks to clean the hole for the kneading shaft should it get clogged with dough.

The bread pan, fashioned from nonstick metal, needs only a sponging with mild soap and water both inside and out. Never leave the case submerged in water, and treat the nonstick coating gently—no steel wool pads or metal implements! Clean the outside casing and the inside of the baking cavity with a damp cloth, taking care to wipe away any stray crumbs.

Never attempt to clean the bread machine unless it is unplugged and completely cool. Store the machine after wiping it clean and making certain it is dry.

TO BAKE A LOAF OF BREAD IN THE BREADMAN

The following times represent the total time required for the entire bread-making process, including mixing, kneading, rising, and baking. At the end of baking, the machine beeps three times and turns itself off.

Basic Wheat, Light setting:	2 hours, 20 minutes
Basic Wheat, Medium setting:	2 hours, 30 minutes
Basic Wheat, Dark setting:	2 hours, 35 minutes
Fruit & Nut setting:	3 hours, 40 minutes
European setting:	3 hours, 40 minutes

TO MAKE DOUGH IN THE BREADMAN

The following time represents the total time required for the dough-making process, including mixing, kneading, and rising. At the end of the cycle, the machine beeps, but *does not* turn itself off. Turn off the machine manually.

Dough setting: 1 hour, 20 minutes

TO KNEAD THE DOUGH

The machine beeps partway through each kneading cycle to indicate it is time to add ingredients such as nuts or raisins, if appropriate for the recipe. If no additional ingredients are called for in the recipe, ignore the beep.

Basic Wheat setting: 20-minute kneading cycle; machine beeps 12 minutes into cycle.

Fruit & Nut setting: 20-minute kneading cycle; machine beeps 12 minutes into cycle.

European setting: 15-minute kneading cycle; machine beeps 7 minutes into cycle.

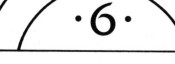

CHAPTER ·6·

THE RECIPES

Without recipes, the bread machine stands idle. With recipes, it can be chugging away daily, baking fresh, aromatic, enticing, and healthful breads for you and your family and friends to enjoy. I have gathered here my favorite delicious, natural, wholesome recipes.

I have divided the recipes into six categories to give you ideas for serving bread beyond the obvious sandwiches and morning toast. There are recipes for hearty whole-grain breads fit for almost any occasion, recipes for breakfast breads, breads ideal for brown-bagging, breads especially good for summertime and picnics, tea breads, and finally, breads for holidays and entertaining. You undoubtedly will think of ways to cross from one category to another, feeling a bread I suggest as a tea bread, for instance, would be just right on Christmas morning or to take as a hostess gift on a summer weekend.

I think this is what baking bread is all about: enjoying the wide variety of flavors, textures, and shapes and discovering creative avenues for integrating them into your daily life. With the bread machine, baking bread is not a once-in-a-while proposition. It becomes part of your everyday routine. But the breads are *never* routine. They are always delicious and always good for you.

TRANSITION AND ELITE RECIPES

I have developed two types of recipes. About 30 percent of the recipes included here are for "transition" breads. The other 70 percent are for "elite" breads. The recipe sections are arranged so that the transition recipes come first.

Transition recipes use unbleached all-purpose white flour. They also include whole-grain flours, whether it is whole wheat or another sort such as rye. These breads are meant to help you bridge the gap between baking with white flour *only* and baking with whole-grain flours *only*. These breads will taste more familiar to those readers not used to whole-grain products. The white flour will seem like an old ally to many, although I predict you will soon be eager to move on to the elite recipes, forsaking nutritionally bankrupt white flour forever.

The elite recipes are those that pull out all nutritional stops. Without question, these are the breads I prefer and believe are the absolute best for you. They call for no refined white sugar, eggs, animal fats, or white flour. They are earthy, full flavored, and bursting with fiber, complex carbohydrates, vitamins, and minerals. Try them all. Quickly, the whole grains and other ingredients will become new and treasured friends.

Since some of the grains and other ingredients may be unfamiliar to you, I have defined them in Chapters 3 and 8. Please refer to these pages before setting out on a shopping expedition. It would also be a good idea to read Chapter 5 on how the bread machine works before you begin baking.

HELPFUL TIPS BEFORE YOU START

I tested all these recipes in the Breadman and in every other major brand of automatic, electric bread machine. While doing so, I jotted down tips that you will find useful as you explore the world of bread baking in a machine. Take a minute to read them.

♦ Be sure to add the ingredients in the order specified in the recipe. Some machines call for the reverse order (dry ingredients first, liquid last) and the ingredients should be put in the machine in the appropriate order. The order is important for efficient mixing and kneading. Most of all, it keeps the yeast and liquid separate until it is time for them to come together.

♦ If you are using the machine's timer, mound the yeast or make a small depression or dent in the center of flour and spoon the yeast into it. This way, the yeast will not sift down the sides of the inner pan and mix with the liquid until the bread machine switches on. This is important for successful baking.

♦ Measure the yeast accurately. Too much yeast can cause the bread to rise too high and then sink. A sunken top can also indicate too much liquid. Reduce the yeast and liquid by half-teaspoon increments if this is a persistent problem with a recipe.

♦ Do not forget to put the yeast in the machine. Odd as it may sound, this is a common oversight.

♦ The water for the Breadman should be warm. This means about 85°, which is not hot but feels warm to the touch.

♦ The other ingredients should be at room temperature.

♦ The most accurate way to measure flour is by weighing it. This method assures that the moisture content of the flour will not affect the amount. I have provided ounce weights for all flour measurements, as well as cup measurements. If you have a scale, use it. Be sure to be consistent: For example, do not weigh the whole wheat flour in a given recipe and then use a cup to measure the rye or corn flour for the same recipe.

♦ If you measure flour in a cup measure, be sure to use a measuring cup designed for dry ingredients (these generally are metal). Spoon the flour into the cup and then sweep it even with the top of the cup, using a blunt kitchen knife. This ensures a far more accurate measurement for my recipes than does dipping the cup into the sack of flour—a practice I do not recommend.

♦ Please note that in the transition recipes, I use all-purpose *unbleached* flour—not bread flour and not bleached flour.

♦ I use non-fat dry milk to tenderize the bread. It has no fat and can be added along with the dry ingredients.

♦ Whey reacts similarly to dry milk. It makes a marked difference in the tenderness of the baked loaf.

♦ I use cholesterol-free egg replacer in some elite recipes and liquid egg substitute in some transition recipes. A *scant* ¼ cup of liquid egg replacer equals one large egg; 4 tablespoons of liquid egg replacer equals one large egg.

♦ When measuring sticky ingredients such as lecithin and maple syrup, first measure any oil called for. This way, the sticky substance slips right off the spoon, which is already oiled.

♦ Lecithin granules can be interchanged with liquid lecithin in equal amounts.

♦ Add ingredients such as raisins, dates, and nuts when the machine beeps for the first time after starting. For the Basic Wheat setting and the Fruit & Nut setting, this is 12 minutes into the cycle. For the European setting, this is 7 minutes into the cycle.

♦ Be sure to use the proper setting for a one-and-a-half-pound loaf or a one-pound loaf.

♦ When using the Dough setting, remember that you cannot use the timer. The machine will beep when the dough is risen and ready to be removed from the bread machine. Press Stop, lift the lid, and remove the inner pan by its handle. Unplug the machine.

♦ Do not open the lid during rising or baking. Instead, look at the bread through the viewing window. Be sure the air vents at the back of the machine are not blocked. Steam needs to escape during baking.

♦ It is fine to open the lid at the very beginning of the cycle. The machine does not perform magic if the ingredients are not in balance. Look at the dough after the initial 15 minutes. If it looks wet, add a tablespoon of flour; if it looks dry, add a tablespoon of water. Let your instincts and your eye guide you—and don't worry too much. Chances are the dough is fine if you have measured carefully. I am speaking of instances when the flour is very moist or the air is very dry.

♦ Take the bread from the machine as soon as it is done (indicated by a beep). If you leave it in the machine too long, it will not cool properly, will lose some flavor and shape, and its texture may be moist and soggy.

♦ Lift the inner pan from the machine using the handle and two hands. In the Breadman, turn the inner pan counterclockwise to loosen it. Don't forget pot holders!

♦ If the baked bread does not slip out of the inner pan easily, twist the blade casing on the bottom of the pan. Use a pot holder.

♦ With some machines the kneading blade may become lodged in the bread. If it does, use a fork, chopstick, or kitchen knife to remove it. Do not use your hands—it is hot.

♦ Let the bread cool on a wire rack. Do not slice into it before it is cool, otherwise the crumb may turn gummy. Use a serrated knife for slicing.

♦ When you make one-pound loaves, the dough tends to gather on one side of the kneading blade and the bread rises in a lopsided fashion. At the end of the kneading cycle (20 minutes for all settings except the European setting, which is 15 minutes), open the lid and look at the dough. If it is unevenly distributed, pick up the dough ball, leave the blade in place, and rearrange the dough in the inner pan so that it is evenly distributed. Close the lid and let the automatic bread maker continue working.

♦ The relatively small quantities of ingredients added to one-pound loaf doughs sometimes cling to the sides of the inner pan instead of mixing together. I suggest checking the dough every five minutes or so during the kneading cycle to make sure the ingredients are mixing properly. This is easy with the viewing window on top of the Breadman. If they are not mixing, scrape down the sides of the pan with a rubber spatula to help the process.

♦ Remove the kneading blade for cleaning. If it does not lift out easily, pour some hot tap water into the pan and let it soak for several minutes.

♦ Clean the blade and the pan gently. They are not dishwasher-safe. Store them completely dry.

♦ Do not forget to replace the kneading blade on its shaft inside the inner pan before putting ingredients into the pan.

♦ Keep your bread machine unplugged except when it is in operation.

♦ Keep the breads fresh by storing them in paper sacks or plastic bags. Crisp crusts turn soft faster when stored in plastic.

High altitude cooking presents its own set of rules because yeast works more effectively high above sea level. There is no hard and fast formula for adjusting the recipes for cooking at lofty heights, but in general, reduce the amount of yeast by ¼ teaspoon for every 2,000 feet. If the loaf has a sunken top, cut back the yeast by another ¼ teaspoon.

The recipes are designed for sea-level baking. As a note of interest, I live at 5,000 feet in Montana and when I make these recipes, I reduce the amount of yeast by ½ teaspoon, regardless of whether I am making a one-and-a-half pound loaf or a one-pound loaf.

The recipes that follow are arranged by category and also are labeled "transition" and "elite." I have put the transition recipes at the beginning of each section and followed them with the elite recipes. As I explain on page 50, transition recipes use unbleached all-purpose flour as well as whole-grain flour. Elite recipes rely solely on whole-grain flours and are the best for you. I also think they taste the best, too! I included the transition recipes as a way to move you gradually away from recipes using white flour. Transition recipes may be a little more familiar to you than the elite recipes and so you may choose to begin experimenting with them before moving on to the elite recipes.

HEARTY
WHOLE-GRAIN BREADS

These are the breads you will bake time and again. They will quickly become part of the family—these are the breads most often found on the supper table, in the bread box, and sliced for toasting. Remember, the recipes called "transition" include some white flour, but those called "elite" are all whole grain. In the latter, I use multi-grain cereals, Kamut, quinoa, rye, amaranth, and buckwheat, as well as whole wheat flour. Some recipes call for sprouted wheat berries, others for rolled oats or bran. The baked loaves are full of earthy, wholesome flavors as well as fiber, vitamins, and minerals. These breads are, for my family and me, truly the staff of life.

OLD-FASHIONED WHEAT BREAD

Transition

Makes one 1½-pound loaf

I begin the recipes with this classic loaf, a nutritious bread that will quickly become a favorite for sandwiches and morning toast.

1 cup (8 ounces) water
2 tablespoons canola oil
2 tablespoons maple syrup
2½ cups (12 ounces) unbleached all-purpose flour
½ cup (2½ ounces) whole wheat flour
3 tablespoons powdered milk
1½ teaspoons fine sea salt
2 teaspoons active dry yeast

Put all the ingredients in the inner pan in the order listed, or in the reverse order if the manual for your machine specifies dry ingredients first and liquids last. Select Basic Wheat cycle, Light setting (or the equivalent setting for your machine, see chart, pages 42–44). Push Start.

OLD-FASHIONED WHEAT BREAD

Transition

Variation for one 1-pound loaf

¾ cup (6 ounces) water
1½ tablespoons canola oil
1½ tablespoons maple syrup
1⅔ cups (8 ounces) unbleached all-purpose flour
⅓ cup (1½ ounces) whole wheat flour
2 tablespoons powdered milk
1 teaspoon fine sea salt
1½ teaspoons active dry yeast

Put all the ingredients in the inner pan in the order listed, or in the reverse order if the manual for your machine specifies dry ingredients first and liquids last. Select Basic Wheat cycle, Light setting (or the equivalent setting for your machine, see chart, pages 42–44). Push Start.

SPROUTED WHEAT BERRY BREAD

Transition

Makes one 1½-pound loaf

*Y*ou *will have to sprout wheat berries to make this loaf. It's easy to do (see box below), but requires a few days' advance planning. Wheat berries are simply wheat kernels, available in natural food stores.*

¾ cup (3 ounces) sprouted wheat berries
¾ cup plus 2 tablespoons (7 ounces) water
1½ tablespoons canola oil
1½ tablespoons maple syrup
2¼ cups (10¾ ounces) unbleached all-purpose flour
¾ cup (3½ ounces) whole wheat flour
2 tablespoons powdered milk
1½ teaspoons fine sea salt
1½ teaspoons active dry yeast

Put all the ingredients in the inner pan in the order listed, or in the reverse order if the manual for your machine specifies dry ingredients first and liquids last. Select Basic Wheat cycle, Light setting (or the equivalent setting for your machine, see chart, pages 42–44). Push Start.

SPROUTING WHEAT BERRIES

*T*o make sprouted wheat berries, put 1 cup wheat berries into 2 cups water. Soak them overnight at room temperature and drain. Put the berries in a loosely covered bowl or jar with a perforated lid. Rinse with fresh cold water and drain again. Rinse and drain the berries twice a day to keep them moist. They will be sprouted and ready to use in 3 to 4 days. Wheat berries, which are simply wheat kernels, can be bought in natural food stores.

SPROUTED WHEAT BERRY BREAD

Transition

Variation for one 1-pound loaf

½ cup (2 ounces) sprouted wheat berries
¼ cup plus 2 tablespoons (5 ounces) water
1 tablespoon canola oil
1 tablespoon maple syrup
1⅔ cups (8 ounces) unbleached all-purpose flour
⅓ cup (1½ ounces) whole wheat flour
1½ tablespoons powdered milk
1 teaspoon fine sea salt
1 teaspoon active dry yeast

Put all the ingredients in the inner pan in the order listed, or in the reverse order if the manual for your machine specifies dry ingredients first and liquids last. Select Basic Wheat cycle, Light setting (or the equivalent setting for your machine, see chart, pages 42–44). Push Start.

OATMEAL BREAD

Transition

Makes one 1½-pound loaf

A thick slice of this homey bread is as comforting and filling as a bowl of steaming hot oatmeal on a cold, stormy morning.

1 cup plus 2 tablespoons (9 ounces) water
1½ tablespoons canola oil
2 tablespoons maple syrup
2¼ cups (10¾ ounces) unbleached all-purpose flour
¾ cup (3½ ounces) whole wheat flour
½ cup (1½ ounces) rolled oats
2 tablespoons powdered milk
1½ teaspoons fine sea salt
2½ teaspoons active dry yeast

Put all the ingredients in the inner pan in the order listed, or in the reverse order if the manual for your machine specifies dry ingredients first and liquids last. Select Basic Wheat cycle, Light setting (or the equivalent setting for your machine, see chart, pages 42–44). Push Start.

OATMEAL BREAD

Transition

Variation for one 1-pound loaf

¾ cup (6 ounces) water
1 tablespoon canola oil
1½ tablespoons maple syrup
1⅔ cups (8 ounces) unbleached all-purpose flour
⅓ cup (1½ ounce) whole wheat flour
⅓ cup (1 ounce) rolled oats
1½ tablespoons powdered milk
1 teaspoon fine sea salt
1½ teaspoons active dry yeast

Put all the ingredients in the inner pan in the order listed, or in the reverse order if the manual for your machine specifies dry ingredients first and liquids last. Select Basic Wheat cycle, Light setting (or the equivalent setting for your machine, see chart, pages 42–44). Push Start.

MULTI-GRAIN CEREAL BREAD

Transition

Makes one 1½-pound loaf

Use *either four- or seven-grain cracked grain cereal. Both are sold in natural food stores, and both make a bread that is super nutritious—not to mention delicious.*

1 cup plus 2 tablespoons (9 ounces) water
1½ tablespoons canola oil
1 tablespoon honey
1 tablespoon unsulfured molasses
2¼ cups (10¾ ounces) unbleached all-purpose flour
¾ cup (3½ ounces) whole wheat flour
½ cup (2½ ounces) multi-grain cereal
1½ tablespoons powdered milk
1½ teaspoons fine sea salt
2 teaspoons active dry yeast

Put all the ingredients in the inner pan in the order listed, or in the reverse order if the manual for your machine specifies dry ingredients first and liquids last. Select Basic Wheat cycle, Light setting (or the equivalent setting for your machine, see chart, pages 42–44). Push Start.

MULTI-GRAIN CEREAL BREAD

Transition

Variation for one 1-pound loaf

¾ cup (6 ounces) water
1 tablespoon canola oil
2 teaspoons honey
2 teaspoons unsulfured molasses
1⅔ cups (8 ounces) unbleached all-purpose flour
⅓ cup (1½ ounces) whole wheat flour
⅓ cup (1¾ ounces) multi-grain cereal
1 tablespoon powdered milk
1 teaspoon fine sea salt
1½ teaspoons active dry yeast

Put all the ingredients in the inner pan in the order listed, or in the reverse order if the manual for your machine specifies dry ingredients first and liquids last. Select Basic Wheat cycle, Light setting (or the equivalent setting for your machine, see chart, pages 42–44). Push Start.

ROLLED GRAINS BREAD

Elite

Makes one 1½-pound loaf

*L*ook *for rolled grains sold as a hot breakfast cereal mix in natural food stores and many supermarkets. A popular combination is wheat flakes, rye, oat, barley, and triticale.*

1 cup plus 2 tablespoons (9 ounces) water
1½ tablespoons canola oil
1½ teaspoons honey
1 tablespoon unsulfured molasses
½ teaspoon liquid lecithin
3 cups (14 ounces) whole wheat flour
¾ cup (3½ ounces) rolled multi-grain cereal
2 tablespoons gluten flour
3 tablespoons powdered whey
1½ teaspoons fine sea salt
2½ teaspoons active dry yeast

Put all the ingredients in the inner pan in the order listed, or in the reverse order if the manual for your machine specifies dry ingredients first and liquids last. Select Basic Wheat cycle, Light setting (or the equivalent setting for your machine, see chart, pages 42–44). Push Start.

ROLLED GRAINS BREAD

Elite

Variation for one 1-pound loaf

¾ cup plus 2 tablespoons (7 ounces) water
1 tablespoon canola oil
1 teaspoon honey
2 teaspoons unsulfured molasses
¼ teaspoon liquid lecithin
2 cups (9½ ounces) whole wheat flour
½ cup (2½ ounces) rolled multi-grain cereal
1½ tablespoons gluten flour
2 tablespoons powdered whey
1 teaspoon fine sea salt
2 teaspoons active dry yeast

Put all the ingredients in the inner pan in the order listed, or in the reverse order if the manual for your machine specifies dry ingredients first and liquids last. Select Basic Wheat cycle, Light setting (or the equivalent setting for your machine, see chart, pages 42–44). Push Start.

THE ORIGINAL RECIPE— 100 PERCENT WHOLE WHEAT BREAD

Elite

Makes one 1½-pound loaf

*T*his ranks high on the list of my favorites. One taste and you will see why: It's loaded with the fresh, wholesome flavor of wheat.

1 cup plus 2 tablespoons (9 ounces) water
1½ tablespoons canola oil
1½ tablespoons honey
½ teaspoon liquid lecithin
3 cups (14 ounces) whole wheat flour
3 tablespoons powdered whey
2 tablespoons gluten flour
1½ teaspoons fine sea salt
2 teaspoons active dry yeast

Put all the ingredients in the inner pan in the order listed, or in the reverse order if the manual of your machine specifies dry ingredients first and liquids last. Select Basic Wheat cycle, Light setting (or the equivalent setting for your machine, see chart, pages 42–44). Push Start.

THE ORIGINAL RECIPE— 100 PERCENT WHOLE WHEAT BREAD

Elite

Variation for one 1-pound loaf

¾ cup (6 ounces) water
1 tablespoon canola oil
1 tablespoon honey
¼ teaspoon liquid lecithin
2 cups (9½ ounces) whole wheat flour
2 tablespoons powdered whey
1½ tablespoons gluten flour
1 teaspoon fine sea salt
1½ teaspoons active dry yeast

Put all the ingredients in the inner pan in the order listed, or in the reverse order if the manual for your machine specifies dry ingredients first and liquids last. Select Basic Wheat cycle, Light setting (or the equivalent setting for your machine, see chart, pages 42–44). Push Start.

WHOLESOME SPROUTED WHEAT BERRY BREAD

Elite

Makes one 1½-pound loaf

*H*ere is a richly textured and lovely loaf to offer your family. Try it for hearty sandwiches. The best!

¾ cup (3 ounces) sprouted wheat berries (see box, page 58)
1 cup plus 2 tablespoons (9 ounces) water
1½ tablespoons canola oil
1½ tablespoons barley malt syrup
½ teaspoon liquid lecithin
3 cups (14 ounces) whole wheat flour
3 tablespoons powdered whey
2 tablespoons gluten flour
1½ teaspoons fine sea salt
1½ teaspoons active dry yeast

Put all the ingredients in the inner pan in the order listed, or in the reverse order if the manual for your machine specifies dry ingredients first and liquids last. Select Basic Wheat cycle, Light setting (or the equivalent setting for your machine, see chart, pages 42–44). Push Start.

WHOLESOME SPROUTED WHEAT BERRY BREAD

Elite

Variation for one 1-pound loaf

½ cup (2 ounces) sprouted wheat berries (see box, page 58)
¾ cup (6 ounces) water
1 tablespoon canola oil
1 tablespoon barley malt syrup
¼ teaspoon liquid lecithin
2 cups (9½ ounces) wheat flour
2 tablespoons powdered whey
1½ tablespoons gluten flour
1 teaspoon fine sea salt
1½ teaspoons active dry yeast

Put all the ingredients in the inner pan in the order listed, or in the reverse order if the manual for your machine specifies dry ingredients first and liquids last. Select Basic Wheat cycle, Light setting (or the equivalent setting for your machine, see chart, pages 42–44). Push Start.

KAMUT BREAD

Elite

Makes one 1½-pound loaf

Kamut is easily tolerated by wheat-sensitive people, and while this loaf also calls for whole wheat flour, this is a good choice for those who try to control their intake of wheat products. Be sure not to buy crispy Kamut breakfast cereal! Buy Kamut flakes. Both Arrowhead Mills Kamut and Organic Harvest 101 Grain Flakes work well in this recipe.

1 cup plus 2 tablespoons (9 ounces) water
1½ tablespoons canola oil
1½ teaspoons honey
1 tablespoon unsulfured molasses
½ teaspoon liquid lecithin
3 cups (14 ounces) whole wheat flour
¾ cup (2½ ounces) Kamut flakes (not crispy breakfast cereal)
3 tablespoons powdered whey
2 tablespoons gluten flour
1½ teaspoons fine sea salt
2 teaspoons active dry yeast

Put all the ingredients in the inner pan in the order listed, or in the reverse order if the manual for your machine specifies dry ingredients first and liquids last. Select Basic Wheat cycle, Light setting (or the equivalent setting for your machine, see chart, pages 42–44). Push Start.

KAMUT BREAD

Elite

Variation for one 1-pound loaf

¾ cup (6 ounces) water
1 tablespoon canola oil
1 teaspoon honey
2 teaspoons unsulfured molasses
¼ teaspoon liquid lecithin
2 cups (9½ ounces) whole wheat flour
½ cup (1½ ounces) Kamut flakes (not crispy breakfast cereal)
2 tablespoons powdered whey
1½ tablespoons gluten flour
1 teaspoon fine sea salt
1½ teaspoons active dry yeast

Put all the ingredients in the inner pan in the order listed, or in the reverse order if the manual for your machine specifies dry ingredients first and liquids last. Select Basic Wheat cycle, Light setting (or the equivalent setting for your machine, see chart, pages 42–44). Push Start.

OAT BRAN BREAD

Elite

Makes one 1½-pound loaf

*T*he combined goodness of oat flour, oat bran, and rolled oats makes this a terrific bread for anyone watching his cholesterol or who simply likes the nutty flavor of oatmeal.

1 cup plus 2 tablespoons (9 ounces) water
1½ tablespoons canola oil
2 tablespoons honey
½ teaspoon liquid lecithin
1½ cups (7½ ounces) whole wheat flour
¾ cup (3½ ounces) oat flour
⅓ cup (1¼ ounces) oat bran
⅓ cup (1 ounce) rolled oats
3 tablespoons powdered whey
2 tablespoons gluten flour
1½ teaspoons fine sea salt
2½ teaspoons active dry yeast

Put all the ingredients in the inner pan in the order listed, or in the reverse order if the manual for your machine specifies dry ingredients first and liquids last. Select Basic Wheat cycle, Light setting (or the equivalent setting for your machine, see chart, pages 42–44). Push Start.

OAT BRAN BREAD

Elite

Variation for one 1-pound loaf

¾ cup (6 ounces) water
1 tablespoon canola oil
1½ tablespoons honey
¼ teaspoon liquid lecithin
1 cup (4¾ ounces) whole wheat flour
½ cup (2½ ounces) oat flour
¼ cup (1 ounce) oat bran
¼ cup (¾ ounce) rolled oats
2 tablespoons powdered whey
1½ tablespoons gluten flour
1 teaspoon fine sea salt
2 teaspoons active dry yeast

Put all the ingredients in the inner pan in the order listed, or in the reverse order if the manual for your machine specifies dry ingredients first and liquids last. Select Basic Wheat cycle, Light setting (or the equivalent setting for your machine, see chart, pages 42–44). Push Start.

SPROUTED SEVEN SEED BREAD

Elite

Makes one 1½-pound loaf

To sprout the combined seeds and legumes, mix together about two tablespoons of each kind and sprout them according to the instructions in the box, page 58. After you make the bread, use any leftover sprouts in sandwiches and salads.

¾ cup (3 ounces) mixed sprouted wheat, lentils, sunflower seed, barley, or millet
1 cup plus 2 tablespoons (9 ounces) water
1½ tablespoons canola oil
1½ tablespoons barley malt syrup
½ teaspoon liquid lecithin
2½ cups (12 ounces) whole wheat flour
¼ cup (1¼ ounces) oat flour
¼ cup (1¼ ounces) barley flour
3 tablespoons powdered whey
2 tablespoons gluten flour
1½ teaspoons fine sea salt
2 teaspoons active dry yeast

Put all the ingredients in the inner pan in the order listed, or in the reverse order if the manual for your machine specifies dry ingredients first and liquids last. Select Basic Wheat cycle, Light setting (or the equivalent setting for your machine, see chart, pages 42–44). Push Start.

SPROUTED SEVEN SEED BREAD

Elite

Variation for one 1-pound loaf

½ cup (2 ounces) mixed sprouted wheat, lentils, sunflower seed,
  barley, or millet (see box, page 58)
¾ cup (6 ounces) water
1 tablespoon canola oil
1 tablespoon barley malt syrup
¼ teaspoon liquid lecithin
1¾ cups (8½ ounces) whole wheat flour
2 tablespoons oat flour
2 tablespoons barley flour
2 tablespoons powdered whey
1½ tablespoons gluten flour
1 teaspoon fine sea salt
1½ teaspoons active dry yeast

Put all the ingredients in the inner pan in the order listed, or in the
reverse order if the manual for your machine specifies dry ingredients
first and liquids last. Select Basic Wheat cycle, Light setting (or the
equivalent setting for your machine, see chart, pages 42–44). Push Start.

LIMPA BREAD

Elite

Makes one 1½-pound loaf

*Limpa is a Scandinavian rye bread redolent with the flavorings of anise, car-
away, and orange. Use this deliciously spiced bread for cucumber sandwiches.*

1 cup plus 2 tablespoons (9 ounces) water
1½ tablespoons canola oil
1½ tablespoons unsulfured molasses
½ teaspoon liquid lecithin
2 cups (9½ ounces) whole wheat flour
1 cup (4¾ ounces) rye flour
3 tablespoons gluten flour
3 tablespoons powdered whey
1 tablespoon carob powder
1½ teaspoons fine sea salt
1 teaspoon aniseed, lightly crushed
1 teaspoon caraway seeds
Grated zest of 1½ oranges
2 teaspoons active dry yeast

Put all the ingredients in the inner pan in the order listed, or in the
reverse order if the manual for your machine specifies dry ingredients
first and liquids last. Select Basic Wheat cycle, Light setting (or the
equivalent setting for your machine, see chart, pages 42–44). Push Start.

LIMPA BREAD

Elite

Variation for one 1-pound loaf

¾ cup (6 ounces) water
1 tablespoon canola oil
1 tablespoon unsulfured molasses
¼ teaspoon liquid lecithin
1⅓ cups (6¼ ounces) whole wheat flour
⅔ cup (3¼ ounces) rye flour
2 tablespoons gluten flour
2 tablespoons powdered whey
2 teaspoons carob powder
1 teaspoon fine sea salt
¾ teaspoon aniseed, lightly crushed
¾ teaspoon caraway seeds
Grated zest of 1 orange
1½ teaspoons active dry yeast

Put all the ingredients in the inner pan in the order listed, or in the reverse order if the manual for your machine specifies dry ingredients first and liquids last. Select Basic Wheat cycle, Light setting (or the equivalent setting for your machine, see chart, pages 42–44). Push Start.

PUMPERNICKEL BREAD

Elite

Makes one 1½-pound loaf

Dark, earthy-rich pumpernickel bread is a favorite for sandwiches and for munching with a cup of hot herb tea.

1¼ cups (10 ounces) water
1 tablespoon canola oil
1 tablespoon unsulfured molasses
½ teaspoon liquid lecithin
2 cups (9½ ounces) whole wheat flour
1 cup (4¾ ounces) rye flour
4 tablespoons powdered whey
3 tablespoons gluten flour
3 tablespoons carob powder
1 tablespoon caraway seeds
1½ teaspoons fine sea salt
2½ teaspoons active dry yeast

Put all the ingredients in the inner pan in the order listed, or in the reverse order if the manual for your machine specifies dry ingredients first and liquids last. Select European setting (or the equivalent setting for your machine, see chart, pages 42–44). Push Start.

PUMPERNICKEL BREAD

Elite

Variation for one 1-pound loaf

¾ cup (6 ounces) water
2 teaspoons canola oil
2 teaspoons unsulfured molasses
¼ teaspoon liquid lecithin
1⅓ cups (6¼ ounces) whole wheat flour
⅔ cup (3¼ ounces) rye flour
3 tablespoons powdered whey
2 tablespoons gluten flour
2 tablespoons carob powder
2 teaspoons caraway seeds
¾ teaspoon fine sea salt
2 teaspoons active dry yeast

Put all the ingredients in the inner pan in the order listed, or in the reverse order if the manual for your machine specifies dry ingredients first and liquids last. Select European setting (or the equivalent setting for your machine, see chart, pages 42–44). Push Start.

WHOLESOME MULTI-GRAIN BREAD

Elite

Makes one 1½-pound loaf

*F*our-, seven-, and nine-grain cereals are available in natural food stores. All are just great in this recipe, and the bread itself is one of my all-time favorites.

1 cup plus 2 tablespoons (9 ounces) water
1½ tablespoons canola or safflower oil
1½ teaspoons honey
1 tablespoon unsulfured molasses
½ teaspoon liquid lecithin
3 cups (14 ounces) whole wheat flour
½ cup (2½ ounces) multi-grain cereal or cracked wheat
3 tablespoons powdered whey
2 tablespoons gluten flour
1½ teaspoons fine sea salt
2 teaspoons active dry yeast

Put all the ingredients in the inner pan in the order listed, or in the reverse order if the manual for your machine specifies dry ingredients first and liquids last. Select Basic Wheat cycle, Light setting (or the equivalent setting for your machine, see chart, pages 42–44). Push Start.

WHOLESOME MULTI-GRAIN BREAD

Elite

Variation for one 1-pound loaf

¾ cup (6 ounces) water
1 tablespoon canola or safflower oil
1 teaspoon honey
2 teaspoons unsulfured molasses
¼ teaspoon liquid lecithin
2 cups (9½ ounces) whole wheat flour
⅓ cup (1¾ ounces) multi-grain cereal or cracked wheat
2 tablespoons powdered whey
1½ tablespoons gluten flour
1 teaspoon fine sea salt
1½ teaspoons active dry yeast

Put all the ingredients in the inner pan in the order listed, or in the reverse order if the manual for your machine specifies dry ingredients first and liquids last. Select Basic Wheat cycle, Light setting (or the equivalent setting for your machine, see chart, pages 42–44). Push Start.

BUCKWHEAT OAT BREAD

Elite

Makes one 1½-pound loaf

Buckwheat and oats team up in this recipe to make one of the most nutritious breads in the book.

1 cup plus 2 tablespoons (9 ounces) water
1½ tablespoons canola oil
2 tablespoons barley malt syrup
½ teaspoon liquid lecithin
2 cups (9½ ounces) whole wheat flour
½ cup (2½ ounces) oat flour
½ cup (1½ ounces) rolled oats
½ cup (2½ ounces) buckwheat flour
3 tablespoons powdered whey
3 tablespoons gluten flour
2 tablespoons oat bran
1½ teaspoons fine sea salt
2 teaspoons active dry yeast

Put all the ingredients in the inner pan in the order listed, or in the reverse order if the manual for your machine specifies dry ingredients first and liquids last. Select Basic Wheat cycle, Light setting (or the equivalent setting for your machine, see chart, pages 42–44). Push Start.

BUCKWHEAT OAT BREAD

Elite

Variation for one 1-pound loaf

¾ cup (6 ounces) water
1 tablespoon canola oil
1½ tablespoons barley malt syrup
¼ teaspoon liquid lecithin
1⅓ cups (6¼ ounces) whole wheat flour
⅓ cup (1½ ounces) oat flour
⅓ cup (1½ ounces) rolled oats
⅓ cup (1½ ounces) buckwheat flour
2 tablespoons powdered whey
2 tablespoons gluten flour
1½ tablespoons oat bran
1 teaspoon fine sea salt
1½ teaspoons active dry yeast

Put all ingredients in the inner pan in the order listed, or in the reverse order if the manual for your machine specifies dry ingredients first and liquids last. Select Basic Wheat cycle, Light setting (or the equivalent setting for your machine, see chart, pages 42–44). Push Start.

QUINOA AND SESAME SEED BREAD

Elite

Makes one 1½-pound loaf

*Q*uinoa *is a super source of calcium, and when combined with unhulled sesame seeds results in a tasty and slightly crunchy loaf.*

1 cup plus 2 tablespoons (9 ounces) water
1½ tablespoons dark Oriental sesame oil
2 tablespoons barley malt syrup
½ teaspoon liquid lecithin
⅓ cup (1¾ ounces) unhulled sesame seeds
2½ cups (12 ounces) whole wheat flour
3 tablespoons quinoa grain
3 tablespoons powdered whey
2 tablespoons gluten flour
1½ teaspoons fine sea salt
2½ teaspoons active dry yeast

Put all the ingredients in the inner pan in the order listed, or in the reverse order if the manual for your machine specifies dry ingredients first and liquids last. Select Basic Wheat cycle, Light setting (or the equivalent setting for your machine, see chart, pages 42–44). Push Start.

QUINOA AND SESAME SEED BREAD

Elite

Variation for one 1-pound loaf

¾ cup (6 ounces) water
1 tablespoon dark Oriental sesame oil
1½ tablespoons barley malt syrup
¼ teaspoon liquid lecithin
¼ cup (1¼ ounces) unhulled sesame seeds
1⅔ cups (8 ounces) whole wheat flour
2 tablespoons quinoa grain
2 tablespoons powdered whey
1½ tablespoons gluten flour
1 teaspoon fine sea salt
2 teaspoons active dry yeast

Put all the ingredients in the inner pan in the order listed, or in the reverse order if the manual for your machine specifies dry ingredients first and liquids last. Select Basic Wheat cycle, Light setting (or the equivalent setting for your machine, see chart, pages 42–44). Push Start.

HIGH-PROTEIN BREAD

Elite

Makes one 1½-pound loaf

*T*he soy flour makes this loaf especially high in protein. For a double jolt of protein and a lot of good flavor, spread a slice with Garbanzo Bean and Cumin Spread (page 258).

1 cup plus 2 tablespoons (9 ounces) water
1½ tablespoons canola oil
1½ tablespoons barley malt syrup
½ teaspoon liquid lecithin
3 cups (14 ounces) whole wheat flour
½ cup (2½ ounces) soy flour
¼ cup (1½ ounces) millet
¼ cup (¾ ounce) raw (untoasted) wheat germ
3 tablespoons powdered whey
2 tablespoons gluten flour
1½ teaspoons fine sea salt
2½ teaspoons active dry yeast

Put all the ingredients in the inner pan in the order listed, or in the reverse order if the manual for your machine specifies dry ingredients first and liquids last. Select Basic Wheat cycle, Light setting (or the equivalent setting for your machine, see chart, pages 42–44). Push Start.

HIGH-PROTEIN BREAD

Elite

Variation for one 1-pound loaf

¾ cup (6 ounces) water
1 tablespoon canola oil
1 tablespoon barley malt syrup
¼ teaspoon liquid lecithin
2 cups (9½ ounces) whole wheat flour
⅓ cup (1½ ounces) soy flour
3 tablespoons (1 ounce) millet
3 tablespoons (½ ounce) raw (untoasted) wheat germ
2 tablespoons powdered whey
1½ tablespoons gluten flour
1 teaspoon fine sea salt
2 teaspoons active dry yeast

Put all the ingredients in the inner pan in the order listed, or in the reverse order if the manual for your machine specifies dry ingredients first and liquids last. Select Basic Wheat cycle, Light setting (or the equivalent setting for your machine, see chart, pages 42–44). Push Start.

AMARANTH SOY BREAD

Elite

Makes one 1½-pound loaf

*T*his *loaf is another one that is high in protein and great in flavor. Amaranth, the ancient grain of the Aztecs, is as good today as it was thousands of years ago.*

1 cup plus 2 tablespoons (9 ounces) water
1½ tablespoons soy or canola oil
2 tablespoons honey
½ teaspoon liquid lecithin
2½ cups (12 ounces) whole wheat flour
½ cup (2½ ounces) amaranth flour
½ cup (2½ ounces) soy flour
3 tablespoons gluten flour
3 tablespoons powdered whey
1½ tablespoons amaranth grain
1½ teaspoons fine sea salt
2½ teaspoons active dry yeast

Put all the ingredients in the inner pan in the order listed, or in the reverse order if the manual for your machine specifies dry ingredients first and liquids last. Select Basic Wheat cycle, Light setting (or the equivalent setting for your machine, see chart, pages 42–44). Push Start.

AMARANTH SOY BREAD

Elite

Variation for one 1-pound loaf

¾ cup (6 ounces) water
1 tablespoon soy or canola oil
1½ tablespoons honey
¼ teaspoon liquid lecithin
1½ cups (7½ ounces) whole wheat flour
⅓ cup (1½ ounces) amaranth flour
⅓ cup (1½ ounces) soy flour
2 tablespoons gluten flour
2 tablespoons powdered whey
1 tablespoon amaranth grain
1 teaspoon fine sea salt
2 teaspoons active dry yeast

Put all the ingredients in the inner pan in the order listed, or in the reverse order if the manual for your machine specifies dry ingredients first and liquids last. Select Basic Wheat cycle, Light setting (or the equivalent setting for your machine, see chart, pages 42–44). Push Start.

WHEAT BRAN BREAD

Elite

Makes one 1½-pound loaf

*E*ating this bread is a delicious way to make sure you get enough bran in your diet. Rye flakes are easily found in natural food stores, but rice flakes may be more difficult to locate.

1 cup plus 2 tablespoons (9 ounces) water
1½ tablespoons canola oil
2 tablespoons unsulfured molasses
½ teaspoon liquid lecithin
2½ cups (12 ounces) whole wheat flour
½ cup (1 ounce) wheat bran
¼ cup (1 ounce) rice or rye flakes
3 tablespoons powdered whey
2 tablespoons gluten flour
1½ teaspoons fine sea salt
2½ teaspoons active dry yeast

Put all the ingredients in the inner pan in the order listed, or in the reverse order if the manual for your machine specifies dry ingredients first and liquids last. Select Basic Wheat cycle, Light setting (or the equivalent setting for your machine, see chart, pages 42–44). Push Start.

WHEAT BRAN BREAD

Elite

Variation for one 1-pound loaf

¾ cup (6 ounces) water
1 tablespoon canola oil
1 tablespoon unsulfured molasses
¼ teaspoon liquid lecithin
1⅔ cups (8 ounces) whole wheat flour
⅓ cup (¾ ounce) wheat bran
3 tablespoons rice or rye flakes
2 tablespoons powdered whey
1½ tablespoons gluten flour
1 teaspoon fine sea salt
2 teaspoons active dry yeast

Put all the ingredients in the inner pan in the order listed, or in the reverse order if the manual for your machine specifies dry ingredients first and liquids last. Select Basic Wheat cycle, Light setting (or the equivalent setting for your machine, see chart, pages 42–44). Push Start.

SPELT BREAD

Elite

Makes one 1½-pound loaf

Spelt is a flour that is often well tolerated by wheat-sensitive people. It makes an outstanding loaf.

1 cup (8 ounces) water
1½ tablespoons canola oil
1½ tablespoons honey
½ teaspoon liquid lecithin
3 cups (14 ounces) spelt flour
3 tablespoons powdered whey
1½ teaspoons fine sea salt
2 teaspoons active dry yeast

Put all the ingredients in the inner pan in the order listed, or in the reverse order if the manual for your machine specifies dry ingredients first and liquids last. Select Basic Wheat cycle, Light setting (or the equivalent setting for your machine, see chart, pages 42–44). Push Start.

SPELT BREAD

Elite

Variation for one 1-pound loaf

¾ cup (6 ounces) water
1 tablespoon canola oil
1 tablespoon honey
¼ teaspoon liquid lecithin
2 cups (9½ ounces) spelt flour
2 tablespoons powdered whey
1 teaspoon fine sea salt
1½ teaspoons active dry yeast

Put all the ingredients in the inner pan in the order listed, or in the reverse order if the manual for your machine specifies dry ingredients first and liquids last. Select Basic Wheat cycle, Light setting (or the equivalent setting for your machine, see chart, pages 42–44). Push Start.

CHAMOMILE BREAD

Elite

Makes one 1½-pound loaf

Chamomile has long been known for its soothing effects on the nerves. It aids sleep and digestion and some evidence points to its abilities to relieve the symptoms of headache, fever, colds, and even asthma. To make the tea, steep two chamomile tea bags or ¼ cup loose tea in 1⅛ cups boiling water for 5 minutes. Strain and let the strong brew cool before using in bread. The flavor will be subtle. For a more strongly scented herb bread, use peppermint instead of chamomile tea.

1 cup plus 2 tablespoons (9 ounces) cooled chamomile tea
1½ tablespoons canola oil
2 tablespoons honey
½ teaspoon liquid lecithin
3 cups (14 ounces) whole wheat flour
3 tablespoons powdered whey
2 tablespoons gluten flour
1½ teaspoons fine sea salt
2½ teaspoons active dry yeast

Put all the ingredients in the inner pan in the order listed or in the reverse order if the manual for your machine specifies dry ingredients first and liquids last. Select Basic Wheat cycle, Light setting (or the equivalent setting for your machine, see chart, pages 42–44). Push Start.

CHAMOMILE BREAD

Elite

Variation for one 1-pound loaf

¾ cup (6 ounces) cooled chamomile tea
1 tablespoon canola oil
1½ tablespoons honey
¼ teaspoon liquid lecithin
2 cups (9½ ounces) whole wheat flour
2 tablespoons powdered whey
1½ tablespoons gluten flour
1 teaspoon fine sea salt
2 teaspoons active dry yeast

Put all the ingredients in the inner pan in the order listed or in the reverse order if the manual for your machine specifies dry ingredients first and liquids last. Select Basic Wheat cycle, Light setting (or the equivalent setting for your machine, see chart, pages 42–44). Push Start.

BREAKFAST BREADS

On these pages you will find an assortment of breads I feel are particularly welcome in the morning. How better to start a new day than with a slice of toasted Raisin Bread, Honey, Granola, and Yogurt Bread, or Maple Pecan Bread? Spread a little honey or nut butter on these, eat a piece of whole fruit and perhaps a bowl of whole-grain cereal, and you are well equipped to face the challenges ahead. On weekends, when you and your family linger over the breakfast table, try sweet, indulgent Honey-Cinnamon Rolls, Orange Rolls, or homemade bagels. With the bread machine in the kitchen, it's easy to say "good morning" with fresh-baked breads. Many can be mixed at bedtime and timed to be ready when you get up. The timer on the automatic bread maker does not work for the Fruit & Nut or Dough settings, as these doughs often include ingredients that can sour upon standing.

HONEY-CINNAMON ROLLS

Transition

Makes 16 rolls

These rolls are one of the reasons so many people loved my Mom's baking. One taste and you'll know why.

Dough

¾ cup (6 ounces) water
1 large egg (or ¼ cup liquid egg substitute)
3 tablespoons canola oil
2 tablespoons honey
2¼ cups (10¾ ounces) unbleached all-purpose flour
¾ cup (3½ ounces) whole wheat flour

2 tablespoons powdered milk
1 teaspoon fine sea salt
2 teaspoons active dry yeast

Filling

3 tablespoons unsalted butter, melted
¼ cup honey
1½ tablespoons cinnamon
½ cup raisins

Glaze

5 tablespoons unsalted butter, melted
5 tablespoons honey
3 tablespoons powdered milk

Put all the dough ingredients in the inner pan in the order listed, or in the reverse order if the manual for your machine specifies dry ingredients first and liquids last. Select Dough setting (or the equivalent setting for your machine, see chart, pages 42–44). Push Start. When the machine beeps after 1 hour and 20 minutes, remove the dough. Turn off the machine.

Place the dough on a lightly floured counter or cutting board. Flatten it out slightly and roll it into a 12-by-16-inch rectangle.

Stir the filling ingredients together until smooth. Spread the filling over the rectangle of dough, leaving a narrow border all around. Beginning at one long side, roll the dough into a cylinder and pinch the seam to seal. Cut the rolled dough into sixteen 1-inch slices.

Butter a 13-by-9-inch baking pan. Combine the glaze ingredients and spread them over the bottom of the buttered pan. Set the rolls in the pan on top of the glaze and cover with plastic wrap or a damp cloth. Let the rolls rise in a warm place until doubled in volume, about 1 hour.

Preheat the oven to 350°.

Set the pan on a baking sheet and bake on the center rack of the oven for 25 to 30 minutes. (Glaze that bubbles in the oven will spill onto the baking sheet.) Let cool for 5 minutes. Invert the pan onto a serving platter and let the glaze drip down the sides of the rolls. Scrape any remaining glaze from the pan onto the rolls. Serve the rolls warm, if possible.

HONEY-CINNAMON ROLLS

Transition

Variation for 12 rolls

Dough

½ cup (4 ounces) water
1 medium egg (or 3 tablespoons liquid egg substitute)
2 tablespoons canola oil
1½ tablespoons honey
1⅔ cups (8 ounces) unbleached all-purpose flour
⅓ cup (1½ ounces) whole wheat flour
1½ tablespoons powdered milk
¾ teaspoon fine sea salt
1½ teaspoons active dry yeast

Filling

2 tablespoons unsalted butter, melted
3 tablespoons honey
1 tablespoon cinnamon
⅓ cup raisins

Glaze

4 tablespoons unsalted butter, melted
4 tablespoons honey
2 tablespoons powdered milk

Put all the dough ingredients in the inner pan in the order listed, or in the reverse order if the manual for your machine specifies dry ingredients first and liquids last. Select Dough setting (or the equivalent setting for your machine, see chart, pages 42–44). Push Start. When the machine beeps after 1 hour and 20 minutes, remove the dough. Turn off the machine.

Place the dough on a lightly floured counter or cutting board. Flatten it out slightly and roll it into a 10-by-12-inch rectangle.

Stir the filling ingredients together until smooth. Spread the filling over the rectangle of dough, leaving a narrow border all around. Beginning at one long side, roll the dough into a cylinder and pinch the seam to seal. Cut the rolled dough into twelve 1-inch slices.

Butter a 10-inch round cake pan. Combine the glaze ingredients and spread them over the bottom of the buttered pan. Set the rolls in the cake pan on top of the glaze and cover with plastic wrap or a damp cloth. Let the rolls rise in a warm place until doubled in volume, about 1 hour.

Preheat the oven to 350°.

Set the pan on a baking sheet and bake on the center rack of the oven for 25 to 30 minutes. (Glaze that bubbles in the oven will spill onto the baking sheet.) Let the rolls cool for 5 minutes. Invert the pan onto a serving platter and let the glaze drip down the sides of the rolls. Scrape any remaining glaze from the pan onto the rolls. Serve the rolls warm, if possible.

Note: Make these rolls in a springform pan, and you will create a beautiful freestanding ''cake'' when the pan's sides are removed.

BAGELS

Transition

Makes 12 bagels

*T*he secret of bagel making is boiling the unbaked dough for a minute before baking to give the bagel a chewy, shiny crust.

1 cup (8 ounces) warm water
1 tablespoon honey
2¼ cups (10¾ ounces) unbleached all-purpose flour
¾ cup (3½ ounces) whole wheat flour
¼ cup (1½ ounces) cornmeal
1 tablespoon powdered milk
1½ teaspoons fine sea salt
2 teaspoons active dry yeast

For glaze and sprinkling

1 egg white, beaten until foamy
3 tablespoons poppy seeds, sesame seeds, dried onions, or coarse salt (optional)

Put all the ingredients except those for glaze and sprinkling, in the inner pan in the order listed, or in the reverse order if the manual for your machine specifies dry ingredients first and liquids last. Select Dough setting (or the equivalent setting for your machine, see chart, pages 42–44). Push Start. When the machine beeps after 1 hour and 20 minutes, remove the dough. Turn off the machine.

Put the dough on a counter or cutting board that has been sprinkled with cornmeal. Divide the dough into 12 equal pieces. One at a time, form each piece of dough into a ball. To do so, one at a time, put a piece of dough on a work surface. Use the sides of your hands to stretch and tuck the edges of the dough to meet underneath in the center. Rotate the dough, continuing to stretch and tuck the dough until it eventually forms a ball. Flatten each ball of dough into a 3-inch round. Put your index finger through the center of each bagel to make a hole.

Put the bagels on 2 lightly oiled baking sheets. Cover with plastic wrap, or a damp cloth, and let rise until almost doubled in a warm, draft-free place, about 30 minutes.

While the bagels rise, bring a large pan of water to a boil. Carefully add the bagels to the boiling water, one at a time, and cook for about 60 seconds, turning once. Remove from the water and drain on a rack.

Preheat the oven to 450°.

Brush the bagels with the beaten egg white and sprinkle with poppy seeds, sesame seeds, dried onions, or coarse salt, if desired. Put the bagels on the baking sheet and bake for 8 to 10 minutes, until golden brown.

BAGELS

Transition

Variation for 8 bagels

⅔ cup (5½ ounces) warm water
2 teaspoons honey
1⅔ cups (8 ounces) unbleached all-purpose flour
⅓ cup (1½ ounces) whole wheat flour
3 tablespoons cornmeal
2 teaspoons powdered milk
1 teaspoon fine sea salt
1½ teaspoons active dry yeast

For glaze and sprinkling

1 egg white, beaten until foamy
2 tablespoons poppy seeds, sesame seeds, dried onions, or coarse
　salt (optional)

Put all the ingredients, except those for glaze and sprinkling, in the inner pan in the order listed, or in the reverse order if the manual for your machine specifies dry ingredients first and liquids last. Select Dough setting (or the equivalent setting for your machine, see chart, pages 42–44). Push Start. When the machine beeps after 1 hour and 20 minutes, remove the dough. Turn off the machine.

Put the dough on a counter or cutting board that has been sprinkled with cornmeal. Divide the dough into 8 equal pieces. One at a time, form each piece of dough into a ball. To do so, one at a time, put a piece of the dough on a work surface. Use the sides of your hands to stretch and tuck the edges of the dough to meet underneath in the center. Rotate the dough, continuing to stretch and tuck the dough until it eventually forms a ball. Flatten each ball into a 3-inch round. Put your index finger through the center of each bagel to make a hole.

Put the bagels on a lightly oiled baking sheet, cover with plastic wrap or a damp cloth, and let rise until almost doubled in a warm, draft-free place, about 30 minutes.

While the bagels rise, bring a large pan of water to a boil. Carefully add the bagels to the boiling water, one at a time, and cook for about 60 seconds, turning once. Remove from the water and drain on a rack.

Preheat the oven to 450°.

Brush the bagels with the beaten egg white and sprinkle with poppy seeds, sesame seeds, dried onions, or coarse salt, if desired. Put the bagels on the baking sheet and bake for 8 to 10 minutes, until golden brown.

ENGLISH MUFFIN BREAD

Transition

Makes one 1½-pound loaf

I love this bread for breakfast, especially with fruit-sweetened conserve. Its light, open-crumb texture is immediately suggestive of familiar English muffins. For a touch of authenticity, sprinkle a little cornmeal on the dough after the second rising.

1 cup plus 2 tablespoons (9 ounces) water
1 tablespoon honey
2½ cups (12 ounces) unbleached all-purpose flour
½ cup (2½ ounces) whole wheat flour
3 tablespoons powdered milk
1½ teaspoons fine sea salt
¼ teaspoon baking soda
2 teaspoons active dry yeast

Put all the ingredients in the inner pan in the order listed, or in the reverse order if the manual for your machine specifies dry ingredients first and liquids last. Select Basic Wheat cycle, Light setting (or the equivalent setting for your machine, see chart, pages 42–44). Push Start.

ENGLISH MUFFIN BREAD

Transition

Variation for one 1-pound loaf

¾ cup (6 ounces) water
2 teaspoons honey
1¾ cups (8¾ ounces) unbleached all-purpose flour
¼ cup (1¼ ounces) whole wheat flour
2 tablespoons powdered milk
1 teaspoon fine sea salt
¼ teaspoon baking soda
1½ teaspoons active dry yeast

Put all the ingredients in the inner pan in the order listed, or in the reverse order if the manual for your machine specifies dry ingredients first and liquids last. Select Basic Wheat cycle, Light setting (or the equivalent setting for your machine, see chart, pages 42–44). Push Start.

HONEY, GRANOLA, AND YOGURT BREAD

Transition

Makes one 1½-pound loaf

*T*his bread combines some of the most appealing ingredients on the natural food store's shelves. You will love it—and it's so good for you.

½ cup (4 ounces) water
1½ tablespoons canola oil
3 tablespoons honey
½ cup (4 ounces) plain low-fat yogurt
½ cup (2½ ounces) fruit-juice-sweetened granola
2¼ cups (10¾ ounces) unbleached all-purpose flour
¾ cup (3½ ounces) whole wheat flour
2 tablespoons powdered milk
1½ teaspoons fine sea salt
2½ teaspoons active dry yeast

Put all the ingredients in the inner pan in the order listed, or in the reverse order if the manual for your machine specifies dry ingredients first and liquids last. Select Basic Wheat cycle, Light setting (or the equivalent setting for your machine, see chart, pages 42–44). Push Start.

HONEY, GRANOLA, AND YOGURT BREAD

Transition

Variation for one 1-pound loaf

⅓ cup (2¾ ounces) water
1 tablespoon canola oil
2 tablespoons honey
⅓ cup (3 ounces) plain low-fat yogurt
⅓ cup (1¾ ounces) fruit-juice-sweetened granola
1½ cups (7½ ounces) unbleached all-purpose flour
½ cup (2½ ounces) whole wheat flour
1½ tablespoons powdered milk
1 teaspoon fine sea salt
2 teaspoons active dry yeast

Put all the ingredients in the inner pan in the order listed, or in the reverse order if the manual for your machine specifies dry ingredients first and liquids last. Select Basic Wheat cycle, Light setting (or the equivalent setting for your machine, see chart, pages 42–44). Push Start.

RAISIN BREAD

Transition

Makes one 1½-pound loaf

*T*his is one of my favorite breads because it is nearly bursting with plump raisins. I add half of the raisins in the beginning of the cycle; these are then finely chopped and evenly and sweetly distributed throughout the bread. The rest of the raisins are added after the dough is kneaded and so remain whole, studding the loaf with delicious fruit.

1 cup plus 2 tablespoons (9 ounces) water
2 tablespoons canola oil
2 tablespoons honey
2½ cups (12 ounces) unbleached all-purpose flour
¾ cup (3½ ounces) whole wheat flour
3 tablespoons powdered milk
1 teaspoon cinnamon
1½ teaspoons fine sea salt
2 teaspoons active dry yeast
¾ cup (3¾ ounces) raisins

Put all the ingredients, except half of the raisins, in the inner pan in the order listed, or in the reverse order if the manual for your machine specifies dry ingredients first and liquids last. Select Fruit & Nut setting (or the equivalent setting for your machine, see chart, pages 42–44). Push Start.

Add the remaining raisins when the machine beeps, about 12 minutes after starting.

RAISIN BREAD

Transition

Variation for one 1-pound loaf

¾ cup (6 ounces) water
1½ tablespoons canola oil
1½ tablespoons honey
1¾ cups (8¾ ounces) unbleached all-purpose flour
⅓ cup (1½ ounces) whole wheat flour
2 tablespoons powdered milk
¾ teaspoon cinnamon
1 teaspoon fine sea salt
1½ teaspoons active dry yeast
½ cup (2½ ounces) raisins

Put all the ingredients, except half of the raisins, in the inner pan in the order listed, or in the reverse order if the manual for your machine specifies dry ingredients first and liquids last. Select Fruit & Nut setting (or the equivalent setting for your machine, see chart, pages 42–44). Push Start.

Add the remaining raisins when the machine beeps, about 12 minutes after starting.

ORANGE-APPLE BREAD

Transition

Makes one 1½-pound loaf

*T*his bread makes fine use of pulp extracted from a juicer after you have made fresh apple and orange juice. If you plan to make bread with pulp, it's advisable to peel the fruit and remove any seeds before juicing.

¾ cup (6 ounces) water
1½ tablespoons canola oil
1½ tablespoons honey
1 teaspoon vanilla extract
¼ cup (2 ounces) orange-apple pulp
Grated zest of 1½ oranges
2¼ cups (10¾ ounces) unbleached all-purpose flour
¾ cup (3½ ounces) whole wheat flour
2 tablespoons powdered milk
1½ teaspoons fine sea salt
1 teaspoon cinnamon
2½ teaspoons active dry yeast
⅔ cup (3 ounces) chopped nuts, such as walnuts

Put all the ingredients, except the nuts, in the inner pan in the order listed, or in the reverse order if the manual for your machine specifies dry ingredients first and liquids last. Select Basic Wheat cycle, Medium setting (or the equivalent setting for your machine, see chart, pages 42–44). Push Start.

   Add the nuts when the machine beeps, about 12 minutes after starting.

ORANGE-APPLE BREAD

Transition

Variation for one 1-pound loaf

½ cup (4 ounces) water
1 tablespoon canola oil
1 tablespoon honey
¾ teaspoon vanilla extract
3 tablespoons (1½ ounces) orange-apple pulp
Grated zest of 1 orange
1⅔ cups (8 ounces) unbleached all-purpose flour
⅓ cup (1½ ounces) whole wheat flour
1½ tablespoons powdered milk
1 teaspoon fine sea salt
¾ teaspoon cinnamon
1½ teaspoons active dry yeast
½ cup (2 ounces) chopped nuts, such as walnuts

Put all the ingredients, except the nuts, in the inner pan in the order listed, or in the reverse order if the manual for your machine specifies dry ingredients first and liquids last. Select Basic Wheat cycle, Medium setting (or the equivalent setting for your machine, see chart, pages 42–44). Push Start.

Add the nuts when the machine beeps, about 12 minutes after starting.

ORANGE ROLLS

Elite

Makes 18 rolls

*I*f you have never formed rolls before, you will find them simple to do—
remember to keep both hands slightly cupped and gently rotate the piece of
dough with your fingertips.

1 cup plus 2 tablespoons (9 ounces) water
2 tablespoons canola oil
2 tablespoons honey
½ teaspoon liquid lecithin
Grated zest of 1½ oranges
1 tablespoon powdered egg substitute
3 cups (14 ounces) whole wheat flour
1 tablespoon gluten flour
3 tablespoons powdered whey
1½ teaspoons fine sea salt
2½ teaspoons active dry yeast
2 tablespoons liquid egg substitute, for glaze

Put the ingredients, except the liquid egg substitute for glazing, in the
inner pan in the order listed, or in the reverse order if the manual for
your machine specifies dry ingredients first and liquids last. Select Dough
setting (or the equivalent setting for your machine, see chart, pages 42–
44). When the machine beeps after 1 hour and 20 minutes, remove the
dough. Turn off the machine.

Put the dough on a well-floured work surface or cutting board. If the
dough seems sticky, knead in enough flour (about ¼ cup) to make it
soft and workable. Roll and stretch the dough into an 18-inch cylinder
and cut into eighteen 1-inch pieces. To form into rolls, put a piece of
dough in your cupped palm. Cover the dough with your other, slightly
cupped hand. Rotate the top hand in small circles, and your fingertips
and the heel of your hand will form the dough into a ball. Repeat with
the remaining pieces of dough. Put the rolls, spaced about 2 inches apart,
on a lightly greased baking sheet. Cover with a damp cloth, and let rise
in a warm place for about 45 minutes, or until doubled in volume.

Preheat the oven to 375°. Lightly brush the tops of the rolls with
the liquid egg substitute. Bake for 15 to 20 minutes, until golden brown.

ORANGE ROLLS

Elite

Variation for 12 rolls

¾ cup (6 ounces) water
1½ tablespoons canola oil
1½ tablespoons honey
¼ teaspoon liquid lecithin
Grated zest of 1 orange
2 teaspoons powdered egg substitute
2 cups (9½ ounces) whole wheat flour
2 teaspoons gluten flour
2 tablespoons powdered whey
1 teaspoon fine sea salt
2 teaspoons active dry yeast
1½ tablespoons liquid egg substitute, for glaze

Put the ingredients, except the liquid egg substitute for glazing, in the inner pan in the order listed, or in the reverse order if the manual for your machine specifies dry ingredients first and liquids last. Select Dough setting (or the equivalent setting for your machine, see chart, pages 42–44). When the machine beeps after 1 hour and 20 minutes, remove the dough. Turn off the machine.

Put the dough on a well-floured work surface or cutting board. If the dough seems sticky, knead in enough flour (about ¼ cup) to make it soft and workable. Roll and stretch the dough into a 12-inch cylinder and cut into twelve 1-inch pieces. To form into rolls, put a piece of dough in your cupped palm. Cover the dough with your other, slightly cupped hand. Rotate the top hand in small circles, and your fingertips and the heel of your hand will form the dough into a ball. Repeat with the remaining pieces of dough. Put the rolls, spaced about 2 inches apart, on a lightly greased baking sheet. Cover with a damp cloth, and let rise in a warm place for about 45 minutes, or until doubled in volume.

Preheat the oven to 375°. Lightly brush the tops of the rolls with the liquid egg substitute. Bake for 15 to 20 minutes, until golden brown.

POPPY SEED BREAD

Elite

Makes one 1½-pound loaf

*T*he hint of lemon marries well with the flavor of the poppy seeds infusing the bread.

1 cup plus 2 tablespoons (9 ounces) water
1½ tablespoons canola oil
1½ tablespoons honey
½ teaspoon liquid lecithin
Grated zest of 1 lemon
3 cups (14 ounces) whole wheat flour
½ cup (1½ ounces) rolled oats
3 tablespoons powdered whey
2 tablespoons gluten flour
1½ teaspoons fine sea salt
½ teaspoon grated nutmeg
2 teaspoons active dry yeast
¼ cup (1¾ ounces) poppy seeds

Put all the ingredients, except the poppy seeds, in the inner pan in the order listed, or in the reverse order if the manual for your machine specifies dry ingredients first and liquids last. Select Basic Wheat cycle, Light setting (or the equivalent setting for your machine, see chart, pages 42–44). Push Start.

Add the poppy seeds when the machine beeps, about 12 minutes after starting.

POPPY SEED BREAD

Elite

Variation for one 1-pound loaf

¾ cup (6 ounces) water
1 tablespoon canola oil
1 tablespoon honey
¼ teaspoon liquid lecithin
Grated zest of ½ lemon
2 cups (9½ ounces) whole wheat flour
⅓ cup (1 ounce) rolled oats
2 tablespoons powdered whey
1½ tablespoons gluten flour
1 teaspoon fine sea salt
⅓ teaspoon grated nutmeg
1½ teaspoons active dry yeast
3 tablespoons poppy seeds

Put all the ingredients, except the poppy seeds, in the inner pan in the order listed, or in the reverse order if the manual for your machine specifies dry ingredients first and liquids last. Select Basic Wheat cycle, Light setting (or the equivalent setting for your machine, see chart, pages 42–44). Push Start.

Add the poppy seeds when the machine beeps, about 12 minutes after starting.

APRICOT NUT BREAD

Elite

Makes one 1½-pound loaf

*F*ew *combinations beat that of apricots and pecans in this moist, flavorful bread.*

1 cup (8 ounces) water
1½ tablespoons canola oil
1½ tablespoons honey
½ teaspoon liquid lecithin
2 tablespoons all-fruit apricot preserves
3 cups (14 ounces) whole wheat flour
3 tablespoons powdered whey
2 tablespoons gluten flour
1¼ teaspoons fine sea salt
2½ teaspoons active dry yeast
½ cup (4 ounces) chopped unsulfured dried apricots
½ cup (2 ounces) pecans, chopped

Put all the ingredients, except the apricots and pecans, in the inner pan in the order listed, or in the reverse order if the manual for your machine specifies dry ingredients first and liquids last. Select Fruit & Nut setting (or the equivalent setting for your machine, see chart, pages 42–44). Push Start.

Add the apricots and pecans when the machine beeps, about 12 minutes after starting.

APRICOT NUT BREAD

Elite

Variation for one 1-pound loaf

¾ cup (6 ounces) water
1 tablespoon canola oil
1 tablespoon honey
¼ teaspoon liquid lecithin
1½ tablespoons all-fruit apricot preserves
2 cups (9½ ounces) whole wheat flour
2 tablespoons powdered whey
1½ tablespoons gluten flour
1 teaspoon fine sea salt
2 teaspoons active dry yeast
⅓ cup (3 ounces) chopped unsulfured dried apricots
⅓ cup (1½ ounces) pecans, chopped

Put all the ingredients, except the apricots and pecans, in the inner pan in the order listed, or in the reverse order if the manual for your machine specifies dry ingredients first and liquids last. Select Fruit & Nut setting (or the equivalent setting for your machine, see chart, pages 42–44). Push Start.

Add the apricots and pecans when the machine beeps, about 12 minutes after starting.

FRUIT AND BRAN MUFFIN BREAD

Elite

Makes one 1½-pound loaf

1 cup (8 ounces) bottled apple juice, at room temperature
2 tablespoons canola oil
1 tablespoon unsulfured molasses
1 tablespoon honey
1 teaspoon vanilla extract
½ teaspoon liquid lecithin
2 teaspoons powdered egg substitute
2¾ cups (13 ounces) whole wheat flour
¾ cup (1½ ounces) wheat bran
3 tablespoons powdered whey
2 tablespoons gluten flour
1 teaspoon cinnamon
1½ teaspoons fine sea salt
2½ teaspoons active dry yeast
¼ cup (1¼ ounces) raisins
¼ cup (1¼ ounces) dates, chopped
¼ cup (1 ounce) chopped walnuts

Put all the ingredients, except the raisins, dates, and walnuts, in the inner pan in the order listed, or in the reverse order if the manual for your machine specifies dry ingredients first and liquids last. Select Fruit & Nut setting (or the equivalent setting for your machine, see chart, pages 42–44). Push Start.

Add the raisins, dates, and nuts when the machine beeps, about 12 minutes after starting.

FRUIT AND BRAN MUFFIN BREAD

Elite

Variation for one 1-pound loaf

¾ cup (6 ounces) bottled apple juice, at room temperature
1½ tablespoons canola oil
2 teaspoons unsulfured molasses
2 teaspoons honey
¾ teaspoon vanilla extract
¼ teaspoon liquid lecithin
1½ teaspoons powdered egg substitute
1¾ cups (8½ ounces) whole wheat flour
½ cup (1 ounce) wheat bran
2 tablespoons powdered whey
1½ tablespoons gluten flour
¾ teaspoon cinnamon
1 teaspoon fine sea salt
2 teaspoons active dry yeast
3 tablespoons raisins
3 tablespoons dates, chopped
3 tablespoons chopped walnuts

Put all the ingredients, except the raisins, dates, and walnuts, in the inner pan in the order listed, or in the reverse order if the manual for your machine specifies dry ingredients first and liquids last. Select Fruit & Nut setting (or the equivalent setting for your machine, see chart, pages 42–44). Push Start.

Add the raisins, dates, and nuts when the machine beeps, about 12 minutes after starting.

MAPLE PECAN BREAD

Elite

Makes one 1½-pound loaf

To bolster the elusive flavor of the maple syrup in this recipe, I add a teaspoon of maple extract with the liquids. High-quality extracts are available at natural food stores.

1 cup plus 2 tablespoons (9 ounces) water
2 tablespoons walnut oil
2 tablespoons maple syrup
½ teaspoon liquid lecithin
1 teaspoon maple extract
2 teaspoons powdered egg substitute
3 cups (14 ounces) whole wheat flour
3 tablespoons powdered whey
2 tablespoons gluten flour
1½ teaspoons fine sea salt
2½ teaspoons active dry yeast
¼ cup (1 ounce) ground pecans
¼ cup (1 ounce) chopped pecans

Put all the ingredients, except the ground and chopped pecans, in the inner pan in the order listed, or in the reverse order if the manual for your machine specifies dry ingredients first and liquids last. Select Fruit & Nut setting (or the equivalent setting for your machine, see chart, pages 42–44). Push Start.

Add the pecans when the machine beeps, about 12 minutes after starting.

MAPLE PECAN BREAD

Elite

Variation for one 1-pound loaf

¾ cup plus 2 tablespoons (7 ounces) water
1½ tablespoons walnut oil
1½ tablespoons maple syrup
¼ teaspoon liquid lecithin
¾ teaspoon maple extract
1½ teaspoons powdered egg substitute
2 cups (9½ ounces) whole wheat flour
2 tablespoons powdered whey
1½ tablespoons gluten flour
1 teaspoon fine sea salt
2 teaspoons active dry yeast
3 tablespoons ground pecans
3 tablespoons chopped pecans

Put all the ingredients, except the ground and chopped pecans, in the inner pan in the order listed, or in the reverse order if the manual for your machine specifies dry ingredients first and liquids last. Select Fruit & Nut setting (or the equivalent setting for your machine, see chart, pages 42–44). Push Start.

Add the pecans when the machine beeps, about 12 minutes after starting.

GOOD-FOR-YOU HONEY AND SPICE RAISIN BREAD PUDDING

Makes 4 servings

Leftover fruited breads, such as Raisin Bread, make superb bread pudding. The healthful, low-fat dessert is sweetened by the bread as well as a little golden honey. I bake the pudding with soy milk and egg substitute instead of cholesterol-rich milk and whole eggs.

4 cups stale raisin bread cubes (from ½-inch-thick bread slices)
1 tablespoon cornstarch
2 cups soy milk, divided
½ cup liquid egg substitute
⅓ cup honey
1 teaspoon cinnamon
½ teaspoon vanilla extract

Preheat the oven to 350°. Put the bread cubes in a lightly oiled 11-by-7-inch baking pan.

In a medium bowl whisk the cornstarch with 2 tablespoons of the soy milk until dissolved. Add the remaining soy milk, egg replacer, honey, cinnamon, and vanilla and mix well. Pour the mixture over the bread cubes.

Set the baking pan in a larger baking pan. Put the pans in the oven and pour enough water in the larger pan to come halfway up the sides of the smaller pan. Bake for 35 to 45 minutes or until the center of the pudding is set. Cool slightly, then serve warm or at room temperature.

BREADS FOR BROWN-BAGGING

Many of the breads in this book are terrific for sandwiches, but here I have gathered some of my favorites. And not only do they make excellent sandwiches, these loaves stand on their own, so with a piece of fruit or perhaps a container of pasta or rice salad, you can enjoy a totally satisfying and healthful lunch at your desk, in the park, or in the schoolroom.

CHEDDAR CHEESE BREAD

Transition

Makes one 1½-pound loaf

*T*his *satisfying bread, tasting deliciously of sharp cheddar, makes for a great sandwich. But it is also delicious all by itself.*

½ cup (4 ounces) water
1½ tablespoons canola oil
1½ tablespoons honey
2 tablespoons dried chives (optional)
½ cup (4 ounces) low-fat cottage cheese
⅓ cup (1¼ ounces) extra sharp cheddar cheese
1 large egg (or ¼ cup liquid egg substitute)
2¼ cups (10¾ ounces) unbleached all-purpose flour
¾ cup (3½ ounces) whole wheat flour
2 tablespoons powdered milk
1½ teaspoons fine sea salt
2 teaspoons active dry yeast

Put all the ingredients in the inner pan in the order listed, or in the reverse order if the manual for your machine specifies dry ingredients first and liquids last. Select Basic Wheat cycle, Light setting (or the equivalent setting for your machine, see chart, pages 42–44). Push Start.

CHEDDAR CHEESE BREAD

Transition

Variation for one 1-pound loaf

⅓ cup (2¾ ounces) water
1 tablespoon canola oil
1 tablespoon honey
1½ tablespoons dried chives (optional)
⅓ cup (3¼ ounces) low-fat cottage cheese
¼ cup (scant 1 ounce) extra sharp cheddar cheese
1 medium egg (or 3 tablespoons liquid egg substitute)
1⅔ cups (8 ounces) unbleached all-purpose flour
⅓ cup (1½ ounces) whole wheat flour
1½ tablespoons powdered milk
1 teaspoon fine sea salt
1½ teaspoons active dry yeast

Put all the ingredients in the inner pan in the order listed, or in the reverse order if the manual for your machine specifies dry ingredients first and liquids last. Select Basic Wheat cycle, Light setting (or the equivalent setting for your machine, see chart, pages 42–44). Push Start.

EASY ONION BREAD

Transition

Makes one 1½-pound loaf

You won't believe how wonderful the kitchen smells when this savory loaf is baking.

¾ cup (6 ounces) water
1½ tablespoons canola oil
1½ tablespoons honey
1 large egg (or ¼ cup liquid egg substitute)
¼ cup (1 ounce) dried minced onion
2¼ cups (10¾ ounces) unbleached all-purpose flour
¾ cup (3½ ounces) whole wheat flour
2 tablespoons powdered milk
1½ teaspoons fine sea salt
2½ teaspoons active dry yeast

Put all the ingredients in the inner pan in the order listed, or in the reverse order if the manual for your machine specifies dry ingredients first and liquids last. Select Basic Wheat cycle, Medium setting (or the equivalent setting for your machine, see chart, pages 42–44). Push Start.

EASY ONION BREAD

Transition

Variation for one 1-pound loaf

½ cup (4 ounces) water
1 tablespoon canola oil
1 tablespoon honey
1 medium egg (or 3 tablespoons liquid egg substitute)
3 tablespoons dried minced onion
1⅔ cups (8 ounces) unbleached all-purpose flour
⅓ cup (1½ ounces) whole wheat flour
1½ tablespoons powdered milk
1 teaspoon fine sea salt
2 teaspoons active dry yeast

Put all the ingredients in the inner pan in the order listed, or in the reverse order if the manual for your machine specifies dry ingredients first and liquids last. Select Basic Wheat cycle, Medium setting (or the equivalent setting for your machine, see chart, pages 42–44). Push Start.

POTATO BREAD

Transition

Makes one 1½-pound loaf

I make this tender, filling loaf with potato flakes, which are easy to find in any supermarket, as well as your local natural food store. Do not substitute mashed potatoes—the moisture content will be off and the bread will not rise and bake properly.

1 cup (8 ounces) water
1 tablespoon canola oil
1 tablespoon honey
1 large egg (or ¼ cup liquid egg substitute)
2½ cups (12 ounces) unbleached all-purpose flour
½ cup (2½ ounces) whole wheat flour
⅓ cup (¾ ounce) potato flakes
3 tablespoons powdered milk
1½ teaspoons fine sea salt
2 teaspoons active dry yeast

Put all the ingredients in the inner pan in the order listed, or in the reverse order if the manual for your machine specifies dry ingredients first and liquids last. Select Basic Wheat cycle, Medium setting (or the equivalent setting for your machine, see chart, pages 42–44). Push Start.

POTATO BREAD

Transition

Variation for one 1-pound loaf

¾ cup (6 ounces) water
1 teaspoon canola oil
2 teaspoons honey
1 medium egg (or 3 tablespoons liquid egg substitute)
1¾ cups (8½ ounces) unbleached all-purpose flour
¼ cup (1¼ ounces) whole wheat flour
¼ cup (½ ounce) potato flakes
2 tablespoons powdered milk
1 teaspoon fine sea salt
1½ teaspoons active dry yeast

Put all the ingredients in the inner pan in the order listed, or in the reverse order if the manual for your machine specifies dry ingredients first and liquids last. Select Basic Wheat cycle, Medium setting (or the equivalent setting for your machine, see chart, pages 42–44). Push Start.

SOURDOUGH BREAD

Transition

Makes one 1½-pound loaf

There is no way to describe just how special and tasty sourdough breads are: tangy and flavorful, but with a hint of mystery. Every great sourdough bread starts with a great sourdough bread starter.

⅔ cup (5½ ounces) warm (100°) water
2 tablespoons canola oil
1 tablespoon honey
1 cup Sourdough Starter (see page 134)
2¼ cups (10¾ ounces) unbleached all-purpose flour
¾ cup (3½ ounces) whole wheat flour
1½ teaspoons fine sea salt
½ teaspoon baking soda
1 teaspoon active dry yeast

Put all the ingredients in the inner pan in the order listed, or in the reverse order if the manual for your machine specifies dry ingredients first and liquids last. Select European setting (or the equivalent setting for your machine, see chart, pages 42–44). Push Start.

SOURDOUGH BREAD

Transition

Variation for one 1-pound loaf

⅓ cup plus 1 tablespoon (3 ounces) warm (100°) water
1½ tablespoons canola oil
2 teaspoons honey
¾ cup Sourdough Starter (see page 134)
1½ cups (7½ ounces) unbleached all-purpose flour
½ cup (2½ ounces) whole wheat flour
1 teaspoon fine sea salt
¼ plus ⅛ teaspoon baking soda
½ teaspoon active dry yeast

Put all the ingredients in the inner pan in the order listed, or in the reverse order if the manual for your machine specifies dry ingredients first and liquids last. Select European setting (or the equivalent setting for your machine, see chart, pages 42–44). Push Start.

SOURDOUGH WHEAT BREAD

Elite

Makes one 1½-pound loaf

Sourdough bread is a favorite in San Francisco—where they love good food. The warm water raises the temperature of the chilled sourdough starter, especially important since the starter is stored in the refrigerator and may not have come to room temperature before you are ready to use it. This recipe combines the goodness of whole wheat with the distinctive taste of sourdough.

1 cup (8 ounces) Whole Wheat Sourdough Starter (see page 135)
⅔ cup (5½ ounces) warm (100°) water
1½ tablespoons canola oil
1 tablespoon honey
½ teaspoon liquid lecithin
3 cups (14 ounces) whole wheat flour
3 tablespoons powdered whey
2 tablespoons gluten flour
1½ teaspoons fine sea salt
1½ teaspoons active dry yeast

Put all the ingredients in the inner pan in the order listed, or in the reverse order if the manual for your machine specifies dry ingredients first and liquids last. Select European setting (or the equivalent setting for your machine, see chart, pages 42–44). Push Start.

SOURDOUGH WHEAT BREAD

Elite

Variation for one 1-pound loaf

¾ cup (6 ounces) Whole Wheat Sourdough Starter (see
   page 135)
½ cup (4 ounces) warm (100°) water
1 tablespoon canola oil
2 teaspoons honey
¼ teaspoon liquid lecithin
2 cups (9½ ounces) whole wheat flour
2 tablespoons powdered whey
1½ tablespoons gluten flour
1 teaspoon fine sea salt
1 teaspoon active dry yeast

Put all the ingredients in the inner pan in the order listed, or in the
reverse order if the manual for your machine specifies dry ingredients
first and liquids last. Select European setting (or the equivalent setting
for your machine, see chart, pages 42–44). Push Start.

SOURDOUGH STARTER

Transition

Makes 2 cups

2 cups (1 pint) warm (100°) water
2½ teaspoons active dry yeast
1 tablespoon honey
2 cups (9½ ounces) unbleached all-purpose flour

Put the water, yeast, and honey in a medium mixing bowl. Let the mixture stand for 10 minutes. Stir until the yeast dissolves. Stir in the flour and beat until smooth. Cover the bowl with plastic wrap and let stand at room temperature for 2 to 5 days, stirring occasionally. The longer the starter stands, the stronger the flavor. The starter will bubble and a sour smelling liquid may form on top. This is normal for a healthy starter, so simply pour the liquid off and discard.

To store the starter, pour it into a sterilized crock or jar. (To sterilize, pour boiling water into the container, let stand 5 minutes, drain, and dry well.) Cover and refrigerate the starter in the jar until ready to use.

To use the starter, stir and pour off as much as required.

To feed the starter, use or remove and discard 1 cup of starter. Add equal amounts (about 1 cup each) of flour (the same kind as originally used) and warm water. Stir and let stand at room temperature until it bubbles again, about 30 minutes, then cover and refrigerate.

To keep the starter from turning rancid, use, or discard, at least 1 cup of the starter every week, then feed it as described above. The starter may be frozen. Thaw in the refrigerator for 24 hours before using. After thawing, pour off as much as required and feed the remainder as described above.

WHOLE WHEAT SOURDOUGH STARTER

Elite

Makes 2 cups

2 cups (1 pint) warm (100°) water
2½ teaspoons active dry yeast
1 tablespoon honey
2 cups (9½ ounces) whole wheat flour

Put the water, yeast, and honey in a medium mixing bowl and stir until the yeast dissolves. Let the mixture stand for 10 minutes. Stir in the flour and beat until smooth. Cover the bowl with plastic wrap and let stand at room temperature for 2 to 5 days, stirring occasionally. The longer the starter stands, the stronger the flavor. The starter will bubble and a sour smelling liquid may form on top. This is normal for a healthy starter, so simply pour the liquid off and discard.

To store the starter, pour it into a sterilized crock or jar. (To sterilize, pour boiling water into the container, let stand 5 minutes, drain, and dry well.) Refrigerate until ready to use.

To use the starter, stir and pour off as much as required.

To feed the starter, add equal amounts (about 1 cup each) of flour (the same kind as originally used) and warm water. Stir and let stand at room temperature until it bubbles again, then cover and refrigerate.

To keep the starter from turning rancid, use at least 1 cup of the starter every week. The starter may be frozen and thawed in the refrigerator for 24 hours before using. After thawing, pour off as much as required and feed the remainder as described above.

WHOLESOME POTATO BREAD

Elite

Makes one 1½-pound loaf

W*hen I have the time, I like using the "real thing" instead of potato flakes. Boil 2 medium-sized red potatoes, unpeeled and coarsely chopped, in enough water to cover by an inch or two, until tender, about 20 minutes. Drain, reserving and cooling the water for the bread. Mash the potatoes with the skins on.*

1 cup (8 ounces) cool potato water
1½ tablespoons dark Oriental sesame oil
1½ tablespoons honey
½ teaspoon liquid lecithin
2 tablespoons dried chives (optional)
1 cup (9 ounces) mashed red potatoes
3 cups (14 ounces) whole wheat flour
2 tablespoons gluten flour
3 tablespoons powdered whey
1½ teaspoons fine sea salt
2½ teaspoons active dry yeast
⅓ cup (2¼ ounces) sesame seeds

Put all the ingredients, except the sesame seeds, in the inner pan in the order listed, or in the reverse order if the manual for your machine specifies dry ingredients first and liquids last. Select Basic Wheat cycle, Medium setting (or the equivalent setting for your machine, see chart, pages 42–44). Push Start.

Add the sesame seeds when the machine beeps, about 12 minutes after starting.

WHOLESOME POTATO BREAD

Elite

Variation for one 1-pound loaf

⅔ cup (5 ounces) cool potato water
1 tablespoon dark Oriental sesame oil
1 tablespoon honey
¼ teaspoon liquid lecithin
1½ tablespoons dried chives (optional)
⅔ cup (5½ ounces) mashed red potatoes
2 cups (9½ ounces) whole wheat flour
1½ tablespoons gluten flour
2 tablespoons powdered whey
1 teaspoon fine sea salt
2 teaspoons active dry yeast
¼ cup (1¼ ounces) sesame seeds

Put all the ingredients, except the sesame seeds, in the inner pan in the order listed, or in the reverse order if the manual for your machine specifies dry ingredients first and liquids last. Select Basic Wheat cycle, Medium setting (or the equivalent setting for your machine, see chart, pages 42–44). Push Start.

Add the sesame seeds when the machine beeps, about 12 minutes after starting.

SALT-FREE POTATO BREAD

Elite

Makes one 1½-pound loaf

*B*ecause many people are on salt-restricted diets, I have included this recipe, but keep in mind that the salt in any of my recipes can be omitted. Salt contributes to a sturdy loaf. Salt-free bread doughs rise faster and may, when baked, collapse a little. When you leave out salt, experiment using cool water and, to strengthen the dough, reduce the amounts of liquid and yeast by half teaspoons. Using herbs in the loaf replaces some of the flavor usually provided by salt.

¾ cup (6 ounces) water
1 tablespoon honey
½ teaspoon liquid lecithin
½ cup (4½ ounces) cooked mashed potatoes (see headnote, page 136)
3 cups (14 ounces) whole wheat flour
3 tablespoons powdered whey
2 tablespoons gluten flour
2 teaspoons dried Italian herb seasoning
2 teaspoons active dry yeast
⅓ cup (1¾ ounces) sesame seeds

Put all the ingredients, except the sesame seeds, in the inner pan in the order listed, or in the reverse order if the manual for your machine specifies dry ingredients first and liquids last. Select Basic Wheat cycle, Medium setting (or the equivalent setting for your machine, see chart, pages 42–44). Push Start.

Add the sesame seeds when the machine beeps, about 12 minutes after starting.

SALT-FREE POTATO BREAD

Elite

Variation for one 1-pound loaf

⅔ cup (5½ ounces) water
2 teaspoons honey
¼ teaspoon liquid lecithin
⅓ cup (3 ounces) cooked mashed potatoes (see headnote,
　　page 136)
2 cups (9½ ounces) whole wheat flour
2 tablespoons powdered whey
1½ tablespoons gluten flour
1½ teaspoons dried Italian herb seasoning
1½ teaspoons active dry yeast
¼ cup (1¼ ounces) sesame seeds

Put all the ingredients, except the sesame seeds, in the inner pan in the order listed, or in the reverse order if the manual for your machine specifies dry ingredients first and liquids last. Select Basic Wheat cycle, Medium setting (or the equivalent setting for your machine, see chart, pages 42–44). Push Start.

Add the sesame seeds when the machine beeps, about 12 minutes after starting.

SEEDED SANDWICH BUNS

Elite

Makes 8 buns

*T*hese may resemble traditional hamburger buns in appearance, but the similarities stop there. My version is good for you and these buns taste so delicious you hardly need a filling.

1 cup plus 2 tablespoons (9 ounces) water
2 tablespoons canola oil
1½ tablespoons honey
½ teaspoon liquid lecithin
3 cups (14 ounces) whole wheat flour
3 tablespoons powdered whey
1 tablespoon gluten flour
1 tablespoon powdered egg substitute
1½ teaspoons fine sea salt
2½ teaspoons active dry yeast
2 teaspoons liquid egg substitute
1 tablespoon poppy seeds

Put all the ingredients, except the liquid egg substitute and poppy seeds, in the inner pan in the order listed, or in the reverse order if the manual for your machine specifies dry ingredients first and liquids last. Select Dough setting (or the equivalent setting for your machine, see chart, pages 42–44). Push Start. When the machine beeps after 1 hour and 20 minutes, remove the dough. Turn off the machine.

Put the dough on a lightly floured counter or cutting board. Cut the dough into 8 equal pieces and form each into a smooth ball. Put the balls, spaced about 2 inches apart, on a lightly greased baking pan. Cover with a damp kitchen towel or plastic wrap, and let rise for about 1 hour, or until doubled in volume.

Preheat the oven to 400°. Brush the tops of the buns with the liquid egg substitute and sprinkle with poppy seeds. Bake the buns for 12 to 15 minutes or until browned.

SEEDED SANDWICH BUNS

Elite

Variation for 6 buns

¾ cup (6 ounces) water
1½ tablespoons canola oil
1 tablespoon honey
¼ teaspoon liquid lecithin
2 cups (9½ ounces) whole wheat flour
2 tablespoons powdered whey
2 teaspoons gluten flour
2 teaspoons powdered egg substitute
1 teaspoon fine sea salt
1½ teaspoons active dry yeast
1½ teaspoons liquid egg substitute
2 teaspoons poppy seeds

Put all the ingredients, except the liquid egg substitute and poppy seeds, in the inner pan in the order listed, or in the reverse order if the manual for your machine specifies dry ingredients first and liquids last. Select Dough setting (or the equivalent setting for your machine, see chart, pages 42–44). Push Start. When the machine beeps after 1 hour and 20 minutes, remove the dough. Turn off the machine.

Put the dough on a lightly floured counter or cutting board. Cut the dough into 6 equal pieces and form each into a smooth ball. Put the balls, spaced about 2 inches apart, on a lightly greased baking pan, cover with a damp kitchen towel or plastic wrap, and let rise for about 1 hour, or until doubled in volume.

Preheat the oven to 400°. Brush the tops of the buns with the liquid egg substitute and sprinkle with poppy seeds. Bake the buns for 12 to 15 minutes or until browned.

HEALTH NUT BREAD

Elite

Makes one 1½-pound loaf

*S*unflower seeds, soy flour, and wheat germ make this one of the best-for-you breads you can make. It tastes great, too!

1 cup plus 2 tablespoons (9 ounces) water
1½ tablespoons canola oil
1 tablespoon barley malt syrup
1 tablespoon unsulfured molasses
3 cups (14 ounces) whole wheat flour
½ cup (1 ounce) raw (untoasted) wheat germ
3 tablespoons soy flour
2 tablespoons gluten flour
3 tablespoons powdered whey
1½ teaspoons fine sea salt
2½ teaspoons active dry yeast
½ cup (3 ounces) sunflower seeds

Put all the ingredients, except the sunflower seeds, in the inner pan in the order listed, or in the reverse order if the manual for your machine specifies dry ingredients first and liquids last. Select Fruit & Nut setting (or the equivalent setting for your machine, see chart, pages 42–44). Push Start.

Add the sunflower seeds when the machine beeps, about 12 minutes after starting.

HEALTH NUT BREAD

Elite

Variation for one 1-pound loaf

¾ cup (6 ounces) water
1 tablespoon canola oil
2 teaspoons barley malt syrup
2 teaspoons unsulfured molasses
2 cups (9½ ounces) whole wheat flour
⅓ cup (¾ ounce) raw (untoasted) wheat germ
2 tablespoons soy flour
1½ tablespoons gluten flour
2 tablespoons powdered whey
1 teaspoon fine sea salt
2 teaspoons active dry yeast
⅓ cup (2 ounces) sunflower seeds

Put all the ingredients, except the sunflower seeds, in the inner pan in the order listed, or in the reverse order if the manual for your machine specifies dry ingredients first and liquids last. Select Fruit & Nut setting (or the equivalent setting for your machine, see chart, pages 42–44). Push Start.

Add the sunflower seeds when the machine beeps, about 12 minutes after starting.

DILL RYE BREAD

Elite

Makes one 1½-pound loaf

*T*he full flavor of dill plays off the equally full flavor of rye in this hearty sandwich loaf.

1 cup (8 ounces) water
1½ tablespoons canola oil
1½ tablespoons unsulfured molasses
1½ tablespoons honey
½ teaspoon liquid lecithin
2½ cups (12 ounces) whole wheat flour
1 cup (4¾ ounces) rye flour
3 tablespoons powdered whey
2 tablespoons gluten flour
2 teaspoons caraway seeds
1½ teaspoons fine sea salt
1 teaspoon dried dillweed
2 teaspoons active dry yeast

Put all the ingredients in the inner pan in the order listed, or in the reverse order if the manual for your machine specifies dry ingredients first and liquids last. Select Basic Wheat cycle, Light setting (or the equivalent setting for your machine, see chart, pages 42–44). Push Start.

DILL RYE BREAD

Elite

Variation for one 1-pound loaf

¾ cup (6 ounces) water
1 tablespoon canola oil
1 tablespoon unsulfured molasses
1 tablespoon honey
¼ teaspoon liquid lecithin
1¾ cups (8¾ ounces) whole wheat flour
⅔ cup (3¼ ounces) rye flour
2 tablespoons powdered whey
1½ tablespoons gluten flour
1½ teaspoons caraway seeds
1 teaspoon fine sea salt
¾ teaspoon dried dillweed
1½ teaspoons active dry yeast

Put all the ingredients in the inner pan in the order listed, or in the reverse order if the manual for your machine specifies dry ingredients first and liquids last. Select Basic Wheat cycle, Light setting (or the equivalent setting for your machine, see chart, pages 42–44). Push Start.

GARBANZO BEAN BREAD

Elite

Makes one 1½-pound loaf

You may know garbanzo beans as chick-peas. Their starch contributes to a light, soft loaf with good keeping qualities, and the beans provide a mildly nutty flavor. Use canned beans, which are already cooked and only need a slight mash, or soak ½ cup dried beans overnight in enough water to cover by 2 inches. Drain well. Cook the soaked beans in simmering water (that has first come to a boil) for about 2 hours, or until tender. Reserve and cool the cooking liquid for the bread. You may use canned beans, reserving the canning liquid.

1 cup (8 ounces) water, from cooking the dried garbanzo beans, or from canned beans
1 tablespoon olive oil
1 tablespoon unsulfured molasses
1 tablespoon honey
½ teaspoon liquid lecithin
1 cup (9 ounces) cooked, drained garbanzo beans, slightly mashed
3 cups (14 ounces) whole wheat flour
2 tablespoons gluten flour
2 tablespoons sesame seeds
1¼ teaspoons fine sea salt
1 teaspoon cumin seeds
2½ teaspoons active dry yeast

Put all the ingredients in the inner pan in the order listed, or in the reverse order if the manual for your machine specifies dry ingredients first and liquids last. Select Basic Wheat cycle, Light setting (or the equivalent setting for your machine, see chart, pages 42–44). Push Start.

GARBANZO BEAN BREAD

Elite

Variation for one 1-pound loaf

¾ cup (6 ounces) water, from cooking the dried garbanzo beans,
or from canned beans
2 teaspoons olive oil
2 teaspoons unsulfured molasses
2 teaspoons honey
¼ teaspoon liquid lecithin
⅔ cup (7 ounces) cooked, drained garbanzo beans, slightly
mashed
2 cups (9½ ounces) whole wheat flour
1½ tablespoons gluten flour
1½ tablespoons sesame seeds
1 teaspoon fine sea salt
¾ teaspoon cumin seeds
2 teaspoons active dry yeast

Put all the ingredients in the inner pan in the order listed, or in the
reverse order if the manual for your machine specifies dry ingredients
first and liquids last. Select Basic Wheat cycle, Light setting (or the
equivalent setting for your machine, see chart, pages 42–44). Push Start.

WHOLE WHEAT PRETZELS

Elite

Makes 12 pretzels

What a kick it is to make your own pretzels! With the bread machine, the hard work is done for you, leaving you with the fun of twisting the dough into the familiar pretzel shape.

1 cup plus 2 tablespoons (9 ounces) water
1½ tablespoons canola oil
1½ tablespoons barley malt syrup
½ teaspoon liquid lecithin
3 cups (14 ounces) whole wheat flour
2 tablespoons gluten flour
3 tablespoons powdered whey
1 teaspoon powdered egg substitute
1½ teaspoons fine sea salt
2 teaspoons active dry yeast

Pretzel bath

3 quarts water
3 tablespoons baking soda
2 teaspoons coarse sea salt

Put all the ingredients, except those for the pretzel bath, in the inner pan in the order listed, or in the reverse order if the manual for your machine specifies dry ingredients first and liquids last. Select Dough setting (or the equivalent setting for your machine, see chart, pages 42–44). When the machine beeps after 1 hour and 20 minutes, remove the dough. Turn off the machine.

If the dough seems sticky, knead in a little extra flour to make a soft dough. Put the dough on a clean, unfloured work surface. Using the heels of your hands and your fingers, roll and stretch the dough into a 12-inch rope. Cut into 12 pieces. Roll and stretch each piece into a thin, 20-inch rope. (If the dough is too resilient to stretch, cover it with a damp kitchen towel and let rest for a few minutes.)

Form each rope into a pretzel shape: On the work surface, form a rope of dough into a large loop with two "legs." The loop and the legs should be equal lengths. Next, cross the right leg over the left to form a twist. Fold the loop down over and past the twist to make the pretzel. This is much easier than it sounds and you will immediately recognize the pretzel shape.

Put the pretzels on a parchment-lined baking sheet. Cover with a damp kitchen towel or plastic wrap and let stand at room temperature for about 30 minutes, until almost doubled in volume.

Meanwhile, bring the 3 quarts of water and the baking soda to a boil in a large pan. Reduce the heat to simmering. Put a clean kitchen towel on the counter next to the simmering water bath. Gently place 3 pretzels in the water. Cook for 40 seconds, turning once with a slotted spatula. Remove the pretzels from the water and drain on the towel for 30 seconds. Return the pretzels to the parchment-lined baking sheet. Repeat with the remaining pretzels. Sprinkle the pretzels with coarse salt.

Preheat the oven to 400°. Bake the pretzels for 12 to 15 minutes, until firm.

WHOLE WHEAT PRETZELS

Elite

Variation for 8 Pretzels

¾ cup (6 ounces) water
1 tablespoon canola oil
1 tablespoon barley malt syrup
¼ teaspoon liquid lecithin
2 cups (9½ ounces) whole wheat flour
1½ tablespoons gluten flour
2 tablespoons powdered whey
¾ teaspoon powdered egg substitute
1 teaspoon fine sea salt
1½ teaspoons active dry yeast

Pretzel bath

3 quarts water
3 tablespoons baking soda
2 teaspoons coarse sea salt

Put all the ingredients, except those for the pretzel bath, in the inner pan in the order listed, or in the reverse order if the manual for your machine specifies dry ingredients first and liquids last. Select Dough setting (or the equivalent setting for your machine, see chart, pages 42–44). When the machine beeps after 1 hour and 20 minutes, remove the dough. Turn off the machine.

If the dough seems sticky, knead in a little extra flour to make a soft dough. Put the dough on a clean, unfloured work surface. Using the heels of your hands and your fingers, roll and stretch the dough into an 8-inch rope. Cut into 8 pieces. Roll and stretch each piece into a thin, 20-inch rope. (If the dough is too resilient to stretch, cover it with a damp kitchen towel and let rest for a few minutes.)

Form each rope into a pretzel shape: On the work surface, form a rope of dough into a large loop with two "legs." The loop and the legs should be equal lengths. Next, cross the right leg over the left to form a twist. Fold the loop down over and past the twist to make the pretzel.

This is much easier than it sounds and you will immediately recognize the pretzel shape.

Put the pretzels on a parchment-lined baking sheet. Cover with a damp kitchen towel or plastic wrap and let stand at room temperature for about 30 minutes, until almost doubled in volume.

Meanwhile, bring the 3 quarts of water and the baking soda to a boil in a large pan. Reduce the heat to simmering. Put a clean kitchen towel on the counter next to the simmering water bath. Gently place 3 pretzels in the water. Cook for 40 seconds, turning once with a slotted spatula. Remove the pretzels from the water and drain on the towel for 30 seconds. Return the pretzels to the parchment-lined baking sheet. Repeat with the remaining pretzels. Sprinkle the pretzels with coarse salt.

Preheat the oven to 400°. Bake the pretzels for 12 to 15 minutes, until firm.

FINNISH RYE BREAD

Elite

Makes one 1½-pound loaf

*T*he whey and the lecithin tenderize and condition this loaf of hearty rye bread. As is the case for many traditional Scandinavian recipes, this loaf is dense, but packed with flavor, thanks to a large proportion of rye flour.

1 cup plus 2 tablespoons (9 ounces) water
1½ tablespoons canola oil
½ teaspoon liquid lecithin
2 cups (9½ ounces) rye flour
1 cup (4¾ ounces) whole wheat flour
3 tablespoons powdered whey
2 tablespoons gluten flour
2 teaspoons fine sea salt
2 teaspoons active dry yeast

Put all the ingredients in the inner pan in the order listed, or in the reverse order if the manual for your machine specifies dry ingredients first and liquids last. Select European setting (or the equivalent setting for your machine, see chart, pages 42–44). Push Start.

FINNISH RYE BREAD

Elite

Variation for one 1-pound loaf

¾ cup (6 ounces) water
1 tablespoon canola oil
¼ teaspoon liquid lecithin
1¼ cups (6 ounces) rye flour
¾ cup (3½ ounces) whole wheat flour
2 tablespoons powdered whey
1½ tablespoons gluten flour
1½ teaspoons fine sea salt
1½ teaspoons active dry yeast

Put all the ingredients in the inner pan in the order listed, or in the reverse order if the manual for your machine specifies dry ingredients first and liquids last. Select European setting (or the equivalent setting for your machine, see chart, pages 42–44). Push Start.

CRUNCHY SUNFLOWER AND MILLET BREAD

Elite

Makes one 1½-pound loaf

The millet gives this nutritious bread its crunch. Make your own sunflower butter by mixing ¼ cup sunflower seeds with ¾ teaspoon canola oil in the blender until smooth.

1 cup plus 2 tablespoons (9 ounces) water
1½ tablespoons sunflower or canola oil
2 tablespoons honey
½ teaspoon liquid lecithin
2 tablespoons sunflower butter (see above)
3 cups (14 ounces) whole wheat flour
2 tablespoons potato flour
⅓ cup (2 ounces) hulled millet
2 tablespoons gluten flour
¾ cup (3½ ounces) raw sunflower seeds
3 tablespoons powdered whey
1½ teaspoons fine sea salt
2 teaspoons active dry yeast

Put all the ingredients in the inner pan in the order listed, or in the reverse order if the manual for your machine specifies dry ingredients first and liquids last. Select Basic Wheat cycle, Light setting (or the equivalent setting for your machine, see chart, pages 42–44). Push Start.

CRUNCHY SUNFLOWER AND MILLET BREAD

Elite

Variation for one 1-pound loaf

¾ cup (6 ounces) water
1 tablespoon sunflower or canola oil
1½ tablespoons honey
¼ teaspoon liquid lecithin
1½ tablespoons sunflower butter (see headnote on page 154)
2 cups (9½ ounces) whole wheat flour
1½ tablespoons potato flour
¼ cup (1½ ounces) hulled millet
1½ tablespoons gluten flour
½ cup (2¼ ounces) raw sunflower seeds
2 tablespoons powdered whey
1 teaspoon fine sea salt
1½ teaspoons active dry yeast

Put all the ingredients in the inner pan in the order listed, or in the reverse order if the manual for your machine specifies dry ingredients first and liquids last. Select Basic Wheat cycle, Light setting (or the equivalent setting for your machine, see chart, pages 42–44). Push Start.

SESAME BARLEY BREAD

Elite

Makes one 1½-pound loaf

*F*or the best flavor, be sure to use dark *sesame oil. Its strong taste stands up far better than light-colored sesame oil.*

1 cup plus 2 tablespoons (9 ounces) water
1 tablespoon canola oil
1½ teaspoons dark Oriental sesame oil
1 tablespoon barley malt syrup
1 tablespoon honey
½ teaspoon liquid lecithin
⅓ cup (1¾ ounces) sesame seeds
2½ cups (12 ounces) whole wheat flour
½ cup (2½ ounces) barley flour
3 tablespoons powdered whey
2 tablespoons gluten flour
1½ teaspoons fine sea salt
2½ teaspoons active dry yeast

Put all the ingredients in the inner pan in the order listed, or in the reverse order if the manual for your machine specifies dry ingredients first and liquids last. Select Basic Wheat cycle, Light setting (or the equivalent setting for your machine, see chart, pages 42–44). Push Start.

SESAME BARLEY BREAD

Elite

Variation for one 1-pound loaf

¾ cup (6 ounces) water
2 teaspoons canola oil
1 teaspoon dark sesame oil
2 teaspoons barley malt syrup
2 teaspoons honey
¼ teaspoon liquid lecithin
¼ cup (1¼ ounces) sesame seeds
1⅔ cups (8 ounces) whole wheat flour
⅓ cup (1½ ounces) barley flour
2 tablespoons powdered whey
1½ tablespoons gluten flour
1 teaspoon fine sea salt
2 teaspoons active dry yeast

Put all the ingredients in the inner pan in the order listed, or in the reverse order if the manual for your machine specifies dry ingredients first and liquids last. Select Basic Wheat cycle, Light setting (or the equivalent setting for your machine, see chart, pages 42–44). Push Start.

WHEAT GERM AND OLIVE OIL BREAD

Elite

Makes one 1½-pound loaf

*O*live oil gives this bread a mellowness that makes it good for vegetarian sandwiches that include roasted eggplant, peppers, and squashes.

1 cup plus 2 tablespoons (9 ounces) water
¼ cup extra-virgin olive oil
1 tablespoon honey
½ teaspoon liquid lecithin
3 cups (14 ounces) whole wheat flour
¾ cup (1½ ounces) wheat germ
3 tablespoons powdered whey
2 tablespoons gluten flour
1½ teaspoons fine sea salt
2 teaspoons active dry yeast

Put all the ingredients in the inner pan in the order listed, or in the reverse order if the manual for your machine specifies dry ingredients first and liquids last. Select Basic Wheat cycle, Light setting (or the equivalent setting for your machine, see chart, pages 42–44). Push Start.

WHEAT GERM AND OLIVE OIL BREAD

Elite

Variation for one 1-pound loaf

¾ cup (6 ounces) water
3 tablespoons extra-virgin olive oil
2 teaspoons honey
¼ teaspoon liquid lecithin
2 cups (9½ ounces) whole wheat flour
½ cup (1 ounce) wheat germ
2 tablespoons powdered whey
1½ tablespoons gluten flour
1 teaspoon fine sea salt
1½ teaspoons active dry yeast

Put all the ingredients in the inner pan in the order listed, or in the reverse order if the manual for your machine specifies dry ingredients first and liquids last. Select Basic Wheat cycle, Light setting (or the equivalent setting for your machine, see chart, pages 42–44). Push Start.

PILGRIM BREAD

Elite

Makes one 1½-pound loaf

The flavors of cornmeal, celery salt, and sage make this loaf reminiscent of Thanksgiving fare. But it is a wonderful everyday sandwich bread.

1¼ cups (10 ounces) water
1½ tablespoons canola oil
1½ tablespoons unsulfured molasses
½ teaspoon liquid lecithin
2½ cups (12 ounces) whole wheat flour
⅓ cup (1½ ounces) buckwheat flour
⅓ cup (2 ounces) yellow cornmeal
3 tablespoons powdered whey
2 tablespoons gluten flour
1½ teaspoons fine sea salt
1 teaspoon celery salt
1 teaspoon crumbled dried sage
2½ teaspoons active dry yeast
⅓ cup (1¼ ounces) dried minced onion
⅓ cup (1¾ ounces) sunflower seeds

Put all the ingredients, except the dried onion and sunflower seeds, in the inner pan in the order listed, or in the reverse order if the manual for your machine specifies dry ingredients first and liquids last. Select Basic Wheat cycle, Medium setting (or the equivalent setting for your machine, see chart, pages 42–44). Push Start.

Add the dried onion and sunflower seeds when the machine beeps, about 12 minutes after starting.

PILGRIM BREAD

Elite

Variation for one 1-pound loaf

¾ cup plus 2 tablespoons (7 ounces) water
1 tablespoon canola oil
1 tablespoon unsulfured molasses
¼ teaspoon liquid lecithin
1½ cups (7½ ounces) whole wheat flour
¼ cup (1¼ ounces) buckwheat flour
¼ cup (1½ ounces) yellow cornmeal
1½ tablespoons gluten flour
2 tablespoons powdered whey
1 teaspoon fine sea salt
¾ teaspoon celery salt
¾ teaspoon crumbled dried sage
2 teaspoons active dry yeast
¼ cup (1 ounce) dried onion
¼ cup (1¼ ounces) sunflower seeds

Put all the ingredients, except the dried onion and sunflower seeds, in the inner pan in the order listed, or in the reverse order if the manual for your machine specifies dry ingredients first and liquids last. Select Basic Wheat cycle, Medium setting (or the equivalent setting for your machine, see chart, pages 42–44). Push Start.

Add the dried onion and sunflower seeds when the machine beeps, about 12 minutes after starting.

SUMMER AND PICNIC BREADS

When the weather is warm and fair we often think of sojourns to the beach, the country, or simply into our own backyards. I have collected a group of recipes that, to my mind, lend themselves to long, lazy picnics, when a slice of bread may hold a ripe, garden tomato, a piece of cheese, or some herbed tofu. These breads taste fresh and light: Many are flavored with herbs, others with summer fruits. I also have included a recipe for making pizza dough in this section, and while pizzas are happy family fare all year long, I think they are especially good topped with luscious vegetables from the summer garden patch. Don't let the heat of the day dissuade you from making delicious, nutritious homemade breads—let the bread machine do the work for you.

BASIC WHITE BREAD

Transition

Makes one 1½-pound loaf

I use only unbleached white flour in this recipe for a high-standing, heartland loaf that is as healthful—and as straightforward—as white bread can be. To make Almost White Bread, you may substitute ¼ cup (about 1¼ ounces) whole wheat flour for the white flour for a boost of nutrients.

1 cup plus 2 tablespoons (9 ounces) water
2 tablespoons canola oil
1½ tablespoons honey
3 cups (14 ounces) unbleached all-purpose flour
3 tablespoons powdered milk
1½ teaspoons fine sea salt
2 teaspoons active dry yeast

Put all the ingredients in the inner pan in the order listed, or in the reverse order if the manual for your machine specifies dry ingredients first and liquids last. Select Basic Wheat cycle, Light setting (or the equivalent setting for your machine, see chart, pages 42–44). Push Start.

BASIC WHITE BREAD

Transition

Variation for one 1-pound loaf

¾ cup (6 ounces) water
1½ tablespoons canola oil
1 tablespoon honey
2 cups (9½ ounces) unbleached all-purpose flour
2 tablespoons powdered milk
1 teaspoon fine sea salt
1½ teaspoons active dry yeast

Put all the ingredients in the inner pan in the order listed, or in the reverse order if the manual for your machine specifies dry ingredients first and liquids last. Select Basic Wheat cycle, Light setting (or the equivalent setting for your machine, see chart, pages 42–44). Push Start.

COTTAGE CHEESE AND HERB BREAD

Transition

Makes one 1½-pound loaf

*H*erbed *no-salt seasoning contributes plenty of flavor to this mouth-watering loaf. Use hot tap water to take the refrigerator's chill off the cottage cheese.*

¼ cup (2 ounces) hot water
1½ tablespoons canola oil
1½ tablespoons honey
1 tablespoon low or no-salt seasoning, such as Mrs. Dash Onion and Herb, or Vegit All Purpose
1 large egg (or ¼ cup liquid egg substitute)
¾ cup (6 ounces) low-fat cottage cheese
2½ cups (12 ounces) unbleached all-purpose flour
¾ cup (3½ ounces) whole wheat flour
2 tablespoons powdered milk
1½ teaspoons fine sea salt
2½ teaspoons active dry yeast

Put all the ingredients in the inner pan in the order listed, or in the reverse order if the manual for your machine specifies dry ingredients first and liquids last. Select Basic Wheat cycle, Light setting (or the equivalent setting for your machine, see chart, pages 42–44). Push Start.

COTTAGE CHEESE AND HERB BREAD

Transition

Variation for one 1-pound loaf

3 tablespoons hot water
1 tablespoon canola oil
1 tablespoon honey
2 teaspoons low or no-salt seasoning, such as Mrs. Dash Onion
   and Herb, or Vegit All Purpose
1 medium egg (or 3 tablespoons liquid egg substitute)
½ cup (4 ounces) low-fat cottage cheese
1½ cups (7½ ounces) unbleached all-purpose flour
½ cup (2½ ounces) whole wheat flour
1½ tablespoons powdered milk
1 teaspoon fine sea salt
2 teaspoons active dry yeast

Put all the ingredients in the inner pan in the order listed, or in the reverse order if the manual for your machine specifies dry ingredients first and liquids last. Select Basic Wheat cycle, Light setting (or the equivalent setting for your machine, see chart, pages 42–44). Push Start.

PIZZA DOUGH

Transition

Makes two 12-inch crusts

Your kids will love helping make their own pizza. Choose your family's favorite topping or use one of mine. Any way you slice it, homemade pizza is great—and so easy with the automatic bread maker. Make this all year long for quick family meals or when friends drop by.

1 cup (8 ounces) water
1 tablespoon extra-virgin olive oil
2 teaspoons honey
1½ cups (7½ ounces) unbleached all-purpose flour
1½ cups (7½ ounces) whole wheat flour
1 teaspoon fine sea salt
2 teaspoons active dry yeast
Cornmeal, for sprinkling
Easy Pizza Sauce (see page 168)

Put all the dough ingredients, except the cornmeal, in the inner pan in the order listed, or in the reverse order if the manual for your machine specifies dry ingredients first and liquids last. Select Dough setting (or the equivalent setting for your machine, see chart, pages 42–44). When the machine beeps after 1 hour and 20 minutes, remove the dough. Turn off the machine. Divide the dough in half and form 2 balls. Let the dough rest for 10 minutes.

Preheat the oven to 450°. Lightly grease two 12-inch pizza pans or sprinkle them with cornmeal to prevent the pizza from sticking.

Using both hands, stretch the dough to fit the pans and press it evenly into them. Pinch the dough around the edges to form a rim. Spread the Pizza Sauce, or another sauce of choice, on the dough and add any toppings. Bake for 12 to 14 minutes, until the sauce is bubbling and the dough crust lightly browned.

PIZZA DOUGH

Transition

Variation for one 14-inch crust

⅔ cup (5½ ounces) water
2 teaspoons extra-virgin olive oil
1 teaspoon honey
1 cup (4¾ ounces) unbleached all-purpose flour
1 cup (4¾ ounces) whole wheat flour
¾ teaspoon salt
1½ teaspoons active dry yeast
Cornmeal, for sprinkling
Easy Pizza Sauce (see page 168)

Put all the dough ingredients, except the cornmeal, in the inner pan in the order listed, or in the reverse order if the manual for your machine specifies dry ingredients first and liquids last. Select Dough setting (or the equivalent setting for your machine, see chart, pages 42–44). When the machine beeps after 1 hour and 20 minutes, remove the dough. Turn off the machine. Form the dough into a ball and let it rest for 10 minutes.

Preheat the oven to 450°. Lightly grease a 14-inch pizza pan or sprinkle it with cornmeal to prevent the pizza from sticking.

Using both hands, stretch the dough to fit the pan and press it evenly into it. Pinch the dough around the edges to form a rim. Spread the Pizza Sauce, or another sauce of choice, on the dough and add any toppings. Bake for 12 to 14 minutes, until the sauce is bubbling and the dough crust lightly browned.

EASY PIZZA SAUCE WITH SWEET RED PEPPER AND OLIVE TOPPING

Makes about 2 cups, enough for two 12-inch pizzas and more than enough for one 14-inch pizza

You may have your own recipe for pizza sauce, but this is one of my favorites. High-quality, sugarless tomato products are available at your natural foods store.

1 tablespoon olive oil
1 small onion, finely chopped
1 clove garlic, minced
1 8-ounce can tomato sauce
1 6-ounce can tomato paste
2 tablespoons water
1 teaspoon dried Italian herb seasoning
⅛ teaspoon crushed red pepper flakes

Sweet Red Pepper and Olive Topping

1 cup shredded part-skim mozzarella cheese
1 small red pepper, seeded and coarsely chopped
½ cup pitted black olives, coarsely chopped

Heat the olive oil in a medium saucepan. Add the onion and garlic and cook over medium heat for 4 to 5 minutes, until softened. Add the tomato sauce, tomato paste, water, seasoning, and red pepper flakes. Cover and cook over medium-low heat for about 20 minutes until slightly thickened.

SUMMER TOMATO PIZZA

Makes one 14-inch pizza

*T*his is a wonderful pizza to make when summer tomatoes are plump and ripe, and your herb garden is bursting with fresh herbs.

1 cup (4 ounces) shredded part-skim mozzarella cheese
1 14-inch pizza crust
4 plum tomatoes, cut into ¼-inch-thick slices
1 clove garlic, minced
1 tablespoon extra-virgin olive oil
¼ cup chopped fresh basil or oregano
Freshly ground black pepper

Preheat the oven to 450°.

Sprinkle the mozzarella evenly over an uncooked 14-inch pizza crust (see page 167). Top with the tomatoes and garlic and drizzle the olive oil over the top. Bake the pizza for 15 to 20 minutes, until the cheese is melted and lightly browned. Sprinkle the basil or oregano and grind the pepper over the top before serving.

CARAWAY RYE BREAD

Transition

Makes one 1½-pound loaf

*T*his is one of the all-time great flavor combinations for bread.

1 cup (8 ounces) water
1½ tablespoons canola oil
1½ tablespoons honey
3 tablespoons minced dried onion
1½ cups (7½ ounces) unbleached all-purpose flour
¾ cup (3½ ounces) whole wheat flour
¾ cup (3½ ounces) rye flour
2 tablespoons powdered milk
1½ teaspoons fine sea salt
1 tablespoon caraway seeds
2½ teaspoons active dry yeast

Put all the ingredients in the inner pan in the order listed, or in the reverse order if the manual for your machine specifies dry ingredients first and liquids last. Select European setting (or the equivalent setting for your machine, see chart, pages 42–44). Push Start.

CARAWAY RYE BREAD

Transition

Variation for one 1-pound loaf

¾ cup (6 ounces) water
1 tablespoon canola oil
1 tablespoon honey
2 tablespoons minced dried onion
1¼ cup (6 ounces) unbleached all-purpose flour
½ cup (2½ ounces) whole wheat flour
¼ cup (1¼ ounces) rye flour
1½ tablespoons powdered milk
1 teaspoon fine sea salt
2 teaspoons caraway seeds
2 teaspoons active dry yeast

Put all the ingredients in the inner pan in the order listed, or in the reverse order if the manual for your machine specifies dry ingredients first and liquids last. Select European setting (or the equivalent setting for your machine, see chart, pages 42–44). Push Start.

TRADITIONAL FRENCH BREAD

Transition

Makes one 1½-pound round loaf or 2 baguettes

*T*he bread machine turns making French bread into an easy affair. Handle the dough gently as you form the loaves. Bon appétit!

1 cup (8 ounces) water
3 cups (14 ounces) unbleached all-purpose flour
1½ teaspoons fine sea salt
2 teaspoons active dry yeast
Cornmeal, for dusting pan

Put all the ingredients, except the cornmeal, in the inner pan in the order listed, or in the reverse order if the manual for your machine specifies dry ingredients first and liquids last. Select Dough setting (or the equivalent setting for your machine, see chart, pages 42–44). Push Start. When the machine beeps after 1 hour and 20 minutes, remove the dough. Turn off the machine.

Form the dough into a ball and transfer it to an oiled bowl, turning to coat the dough with oil. Cover the bowl with a damp kitchen towel or plastic wrap. Let it stand at warm room temperature for 45 to 60 minutes, until doubled in volume.

To make a round loaf: Put the dough on a clean, unfloured work surface. Using the sides of your hands, tuck and stretch the sides of the dough underneath its mass, rotating the dough at the same time to form a taut, smooth ball. Put the ball on a cornmeal-dusted baking sheet and let stand at warm room temperature for 45 to 60 minutes, until almost doubled in volume. Using a sharp, single-edged razor or a very sharp knife, slash an ⅛-inch-deep cross in the top of the risen dough.

To make baguettes: Divide the dough into 2 equal pieces. On a clean, unfloured work surface, roll and stretch each piece into a 14-inch log. Put the logs on a cornmeal-dusted baking sheet. Cover with a damp kitchen towel or plastic wrap for about 45 minutes or until almost doubled in volume. Using a sharp, single-edged razor or thin-bladed knife, make three ⅛-inch-deep slashes on the top of each baguette.

Preheat the oven to 450°.

Quickly spray the inside of the oven thoroughly with a water mister. The resulting steam gives the bread a crisp crust. Bake the bread until it sounds hollow when tapped underneath, about 20 minutes for the round loaf and about 15 minutes for the baguettes.

Note: You may also bake a loaf right in the machine: Put all of the ingredients, except the cornmeal, which is deleted, in the inner pan in the order listed, or in the reverse order if the manual for your machine specifies dry ingredients first and liquids last. Select European setting (or the equivalent setting for your machine, see chart, pages 42–44). Push Start.

TRADITIONAL FRENCH BREAD

Transition

Variation for one 1-pound round loaf or 2 small baguettes

¾ cup (6 ounces) water
2 cups (9½ ounces) unbleached all-purpose flour
1 teaspoon fine sea salt
1½ teaspoons active dry yeast
Cornmeal, for dusting pan

Put all the ingredients, except the cornmeal, in the inner pan in the order listed, or in the reverse order if the manual for your machine specifies dry ingredients first and liquids last. Select Dough setting (or the equivalent setting for your machine, see chart, pages 42–44). Push Start. When the machine beeps after 1 hour and 20 minutes, remove the dough. Turn off the machine.

Form the dough into a ball and transfer it to an oiled bowl, turning to coat the dough with oil. Cover the bowl with a damp kitchen towel or plastic wrap. Let it stand at warm room temperature for 45 to 60 minutes, until doubled in volume.

To make a round loaf: Put the dough on a clean, unfloured work surface. Using the sides of your hands, tuck and stretch the sides of the dough underneath its mass, rotating the dough at the same time to form a taut, smooth ball. Put the ball on a cornmeal-dusted baking sheet and let stand at warm room temperature for 45 to 60 minutes, until almost doubled in volume. Using a sharp, single-edged razor or a very sharp knife, slash an ⅛-inch-deep cross in the top of the risen dough.

To make baguettes: Divide the dough into 2 equal pieces. On a clean, unfloured work surface, roll and stretch each piece into an 11-inch log. Put the logs on a cornmeal-dusted baking sheet. Cover with a damp kitchen towel or plastic wrap for about 45 minutes or until almost doubled in volume. Using a sharp, single-edged razor or thin-bladed knife, make three ⅛-inch-deep slashes on the top of each baguette.

Preheat the over to 450°.

Quickly spray the inside of the oven thoroughly with a water mister.

The resulting steam gives the bread a crisp crust. Bake the bread until it sounds hollow when tapped underneath: about 20 minutes for the round loaf and about 15 minutes for the baguettes.

Note: You may also bake a loaf right in the machine. See note, page 173, for instructions.

BLUEBERRY LEMON BREAD

Transition

Makes one 1½-pound loaf

*T*his bread tastes as fresh and bright as a summer morning. Do not substitute fresh blueberries for dried as they contain too much liquid and will disrupt the balance of ingredients. Dried blueberries are available in natural food stores and specialty shops.

¾ cup plus 2 tablespoons (7 ounces) water
1½ tablespoons canola oil
1½ tablespoons honey
Grated zest of 1 lemon
3 tablespoons all-fruit blueberry spread
2½ cups (12 ounces) unbleached all-purpose flour
¾ cup (3½ ounces) whole wheat flour
2 tablespoons powdered milk
1½ teaspoons fine sea salt
2½ teaspoons active dry yeast
½ cup (1½ ounces) dried blueberries

Put all the ingredients, except the dried blueberries, in the inner pan in the order listed, or in the reverse order if the manual for your machine specifies dry ingredients first and liquids last. Select European setting (or the equivalent setting for your machine, see chart, pages 42–44). Push Start.

Add the dried blueberries when the machine beeps, about 7 minutes after starting.

BLUEBERRY LEMON BREAD

Transition

Variation for one 1-pound loaf

⅔ cup (5½ ounces) water
1 tablespoon canola oil
1 tablespoon honey
Grated zest of ½ lemon
2 tablespoons all-fruit blueberry spread
1½ cups (7 ounces) unbleached all-purpose flour
½ cup (2¼ ounces) whole wheat flour
1½ tablespoons powdered milk
1 teaspoon fine sea salt
2 teaspoons active dry yeast
⅓ cup (1 ounce) dried blueberries

Put all the ingredients, except the dried blueberries, in the inner pan in the order listed, or in the reverse order if the manual for your machine specifies dry ingredients first and liquids last. Select European setting (or the equivalent setting for your machine, see chart, pages 42–44). Push Start.

Add the dried blueberries when the machine beeps, about 7 minutes after starting.

CARAWAY ONION BREAD

Elite

Makes one 1½-pound loaf

This full-bodied loaf is a terrific bread for hearty summer sandwiches.

1 cup plus 2 tablespoons (9 ounces) water
1½ tablespoons canola oil
1½ tablespoons unsulfured molasses or Sucanat
½ teaspoon liquid lecithin
2¼ cups (10¾ ounces) whole wheat flour
¾ cup (3½ ounces) rye flour
¼ cup (1 ounce) dried minced onion
3 tablespoons potato flour
3 tablespoons powdered whey
2 tablespoons gluten flour
1 tablespoon carob powder
1 tablespoon caraway seeds
1 teaspoon dried dillweed
1½ teaspoons fine sea salt
2½ teaspoons active dry yeast

Put all the ingredients in the inner pan in the order listed, or in the reverse order if the manual for your machine specifies dry ingredients first and liquids last. Select European setting (or the equivalent setting for your machine, see chart, pages 42–44). Push Start.

Note: If using Sucanat, you may have to add about 1 tablespoon additional water.

CARAWAY ONION BREAD

Elite

Variation for one 1-pound loaf

¾ cup (6 ounces) water
1 tablespoon canola oil
1 tablespoon unsulfured molasses or Sucanat
¼ teaspoon liquid lecithin
1½ cups (7½ ounces) whole wheat flour
½ cup (2½ ounces) rye flour
3 tablespoons dried minced onion
2 tablespoons potato flour
2 tablespoons powdered whey
1½ tablespoons gluten flour
2 teaspoons carob powder
2 teaspoons caraway seeds
¾ teaspoon dried dillweed
1 teaspoon fine sea salt
2 teaspoons active dry yeast

Put all the ingredients in the inner pan in the order listed, or in the reverse order if the manual for your machine specifies dry ingredients first and liquids last. Select European setting (or the equivalent setting for your machine, see chart, pages 42–44). Push Start.

CORNMEAL HERB BREAD

Elite

Makes one 1½-pound loaf

*B*asil, dill, and sage conspire with poppy seeds and onions to make this one of the most aromatic breads in this collection.

1¼ cups (10 ounces) water
1½ tablespoons olive oil
1½ tablespoons honey
½ teaspoon liquid lecithin
3 cups (14 ounces) whole wheat flour
¾ cup (4½ ounces) cornmeal
3 tablespoons powdered whey
2 tablespoons gluten flour
2 tablespoons dried minced onion
1 tablespoon poppy seeds
½ teaspoon dried sage
½ teaspoon dried basil, crushed
¼ teaspoon dried dillweed
1¾ teaspoons fine sea salt
2½ teaspoons active dry yeast

Put all the ingredients in the inner pan in the order listed, or in the reverse order if the manual for your machine specifies dry ingredients first and liquids last. Select Basic Wheat cycle, Light setting (or the equivalent setting for your machine, see chart, pages 42–44). Push Start.

CORNMEAL HERB BREAD

Elite

Variation for one 1-pound loaf

¾ cup plus 2 tablespoons (7 ounces) water
1 tablespoon olive oil
1 tablespoon honey
¼ teaspoon liquid lecithin
2 cups (9½ ounces) whole wheat flour
½ cup (3 ounces) cornmeal
2 tablespoons powdered whey
1½ tablespoons gluten flour
1½ tablespoons dried minced onion
2 teaspoons poppy seeds
¼ teaspoon dried sage
¼ teaspoon dried basil, crushed
⅛ teaspoon dried dillweed
1¼ teaspoons fine sea salt
2 teaspoons active dry yeast

Put all the ingredients in the inner pan in the order listed, or in the reverse order if the manual for your machine specifies dry ingredients first and liquids last. Select Basic Wheat cycle, Light setting (or the equivalent setting for your machine, see chart, pages 42–44). Push Start.

HONEY AND FLAXSEED BREAD

Elite

Makes one 1½-pound loaf

*T*his slightly sweet loaf is a good companion on a country picnic.

1 cup plus 2 tablespoons (9 ounces) water
1½ tablespoons flaxseed or canola oil
3 tablespoons honey
½ teaspoon liquid lecithin
3 cups (14 ounces) whole wheat flour
½ cup (2½ ounces) whole flaxseed
2 tablespoons gluten flour
3 tablespoons powdered whey
1½ teaspoons fine sea salt
2 teaspoons active dry yeast

Put all the ingredients in the inner pan in the order listed, or in the reverse order if the manual for your machine specifies dry ingredients first and liquids last. Select Basic Wheat cycle, Light setting (or the equivalent setting for your machine, see chart, pages 42–44). Push Start.

HONEY AND FLAXSEED BREAD

Elite

Variation for one 1-pound loaf

¾ cup (6 ounces) water
1 tablespoon flaxseed or canola oil
2 tablespoons honey
¼ teaspoon liquid lecithin
2 cups (9½ ounces) whole wheat flour
⅓ cup (1¾ ounces) whole flaxseed
1½ tablespoons gluten flour
2 tablespoons powdered whey
1 teaspoon fine sea salt
1½ teaspoons active dry yeast

Put all the ingredients in the inner pan in the order listed, or in the reverse order if the manual for your machine specifies dry ingredients first and liquids last. Select Basic Wheat cycle, Light setting (or the equivalent setting for your machine, see chart, pages 42–44). Push Start.

ITALIAN HERB BREAD

Elite

Makes one 1½-pound loaf

I love the the full-bodied flavors of onion and garlic so apparent in this bread. Toast cubes of this bread in a 350° oven to make excellent croutons for your salads.

1 cup plus 2 tablespoons (9 ounces) water
3 tablespoons extra-virgin olive oil
1 tablespoon honey
½ teaspoon liquid lecithin
3 cups (14 ounces) whole wheat flour
3 tablespoons powdered whey
2 tablespoons gluten flour
3 tablespoons dried minced onion
1 tablespoon dried chives (optional)
1½ teaspoons fine sea salt
1 teaspoon garlic powder
1 teaspoon dried oregano
½ teaspoon dried basil, crushed
2 teaspoons active dry yeast

Put all the ingredients in the inner pan in the order listed, or in the reverse order if the manual for your machine specifies dry ingredients first and liquids last. Select Basic Wheat cycle, Light setting (or the equivalent setting for your machine, see chart, pages 42–44). Push Start.

ITALIAN HERB BREAD

Elite

Variation for one 1-pound loaf

¾ cup (6 ounces) water
2 tablespoons extra-virgin olive oil
2 teaspoons honey
¼ teaspoon liquid lecithin
2 cups (9½ ounces) whole wheat flour
2 tablespoons powdered whey
1½ tablespoons gluten flour
2 tablespoons dried minced onion
2 teaspoons dried chives (optional)
1 teaspoon fine sea salt
¾ teaspoon garlic powder
¾ teaspoon dried oregano
¼ teaspoon dried basil, crushed
1½ teaspoons active dry yeast

Put all the ingredients in the inner pan in the order listed, or in the reverse order if the manual for your machine specifies dry ingredients first and liquids last. Select Basic Wheat cycle, Light setting (or the equivalent setting for your machine, see chart, pages 42–44). Push Start.

TOFU CHEESE AND CHIVE BREAD

Elite

Makes one 1½-pound loaf

Tofu cheese is a dairy-free substitute found in well-stocked natural food stores. It comes in an array of flavors, but I prefer the assertiveness of the "smoky cheddar" variety in this loaf.

¾ cup plus 2 tablespoons (7 ounces) water
1½ tablespoons canola oil
1½ tablespoons honey
½ teaspoon liquid lecithin
1 cup (4 ounces) shredded, grated tofu cheese, preferably smoked cheddar flavor
3 cups (14 ounces) whole wheat flour
3 tablespoons powdered whey
2 tablespoons gluten flour
2 tablespoons dried chives
2 teaspoons powdered egg substitute
1½ teaspoons fine sea salt
½ teaspoon garlic powder
2 teaspoons active dry yeast

Put all the ingredients in the inner pan in the order listed, or in the reverse order if the manual for your machine specifies dry ingredients first and liquids last. Select Basic Wheat cycle, Light setting (or the equivalent setting for your machine, see chart, pages 42–44). Push Start.

TOFU CHEESE AND CHIVE BREAD

Elite

Variation for one 1-pound loaf

½ cup (4 ounces) water
1 tablespoon canola oil
1 tablespoon honey
¼ teaspoon liquid lecithin
¾ cup (3 ounces) shredded tofu cheese, preferably smoked
  cheddar flavor
2 cups (9½ ounces) whole wheat flour
2 tablespoons powdered whey
1½ tablespoons gluten flour
1½ tablespoons dried chives
1½ teaspoons powdered egg substitute
1 teaspoon fine sea salt
¼ teaspoon garlic powder
1½ teaspoons active dry yeast

Put all the ingredients in the inner pan in the order listed, or in the reverse order if the manual for your machine specifies dry ingredients first and liquids last. Select Basic Wheat cycle, Light setting (or the equivalent setting for your machine, see chart, pages 42–44). Push Start.

ONION THYME BREAD

Elite

Makes one 1½-pound loaf

*T*his is a terrific end-of-summer bread, rich and earthy with the flavors of the late August garden.

1¼ cups (10 ounces) water
1½ tablespoons canola oil
1½ tablespoons honey
½ teaspoon liquid lecithin
⅓ cup (1¼ ounces) dried minced onion
3 cups (14 ounces) whole wheat flour
2 tablespoons gluten flour
3 tablespoons powdered whey
1½ teaspoons fine sea salt
1 teaspoon dried thyme
2½ teaspoons active dry yeast

Put all the ingredients in the inner pan in the order listed, or in the reverse order if the manual for your machine specifies dry ingredients first and liquids last. Select Basic Wheat cycle, Light setting (or the equivalent setting for your machine, see chart, pages 42–44). Push Start.

ONION THYME BREAD

Elite

Variation for one 1-pound loaf

¾ cup (6 ounces) water
1 tablespoon canola oil
1 tablespoon honey
¼ teaspoon liquid lecithin
¼ cup (1 ounce) dried minced onion
2 cups (9½ ounces) whole wheat flour
1½ tablespoons gluten flour
2 tablespoons powdered whey
1 teaspoon fine sea salt
¾ teaspoon dried thyme
2 teaspoons active dry yeast

Put all the ingredients in the inner pan in the order listed, or in the reverse order if the manual for your machine specifies dry ingredients first and liquids last. Select Basic Wheat cycle, Light setting (or the equivalent setting for your machine, see chart, pages 42–44). Push Start.

JALAPEÑO CORN BREAD

Elite

Makes one 1½-pound loaf

I like the sharp flavor of hot jalapeño peppers, but if you prefer a milder taste, substitute canned green chilis.

1 cup (8 ounces) water
1½ tablespoons extra-virgin olive oil
2 tablespoons honey
½ teaspoon liquid lecithin
½ cup (2 ounces) shredded tofu cheese, preferably smoked cheddar flavor
2 tablespoons seeded and finely chopped jalapeño peppers
2 tablespoons dried minced onion
2½ cups (12 ounces) whole wheat flour
¾ cup (4½ ounces) blue or yellow cornmeal
3 tablespoons powdered whey
2 tablespoons gluten flour
1½ teaspoons fine sea salt
1 teaspoon garlic powder
2½ teaspoons active dry yeast

Put all the ingredients in the inner pan in the order listed, or in the reverse order if the manual for your machine specifies dry ingredients first and liquids last. Select Basic Wheat cycle, Light setting (or the equivalent setting for your machine, see chart, pages 42–44). Push Start.

JALAPEÑO CORN BREAD

Elite

Variation for one 1-pound loaf

¾ cup (6 ounces) water
1 tablespoon extra-virgin olive oil
1½ tablespoons honey
¼ teaspoon liquid lecithin
⅓ cup (1½ ounces) shredded tofu cheese, preferably smoked
   cheddar flavor
1½ tablespoons seeded and finely chopped jalapeño peppers
1½ tablespoons dried minced onion
1¾ cups (8¾ ounces) whole wheat flour
½ cup (3 ounces) blue or yellow cornmeal
2 tablespoons powdered whey
1½ tablespoons gluten flour
1 teaspoon fine sea salt
¾ teaspoon garlic powder
2 teaspoons active dry yeast

Put all the ingredients in the inner pan in the order listed, or in the reverse order if the manual for your machine specifies dry ingredients first and liquids last. Select Basic Wheat cycle, Light setting (or the equivalent setting for your machine, see chart, page 42–44). Push Start.

WHOLE WHEAT BAGUETTES

Elite

Makes 4 baguettes

*F*rench-style baguettes made with whole wheat flour alone taste richer than more traditional baguettes. In my opinion, they rate four stars!

1¼ cups (10 ounces) water
3 cups (14 ounces) whole wheat flour
3 tablespoons gluten flour
1½ teaspoons fine sea salt
2 teaspoons active dry yeast
Cornmeal, for dusting

Put all the ingredients, except the cornmeal, in the inner pan in the order listed, or in the reverse order if the manual for your machine specifies dry ingredients first and liquids last. Select Dough setting (or the equivalent setting for your machine, see chart, pages 42–44). Push Start. When the machine beeps after 1 hour and 20 minutes, remove the dough. Turn off the machine.

Form the dough into a ball and transfer it to an oiled bowl, turning to coat the dough with oil. Cover the bowl with a damp kitchen towel or plastic wrap. Let it stand at warm room temperature for 45 to 60 minutes, until doubled in volume.

Divide the dough into 4 equal pieces. On a clean, unfloured work surface, roll and stretch each piece into a 7- to 8-inch log. Put the logs on a cornmeal-dusted baking sheet. Cover with a damp kitchen towel or plastic wrap and let stand for about 45 minutes or until almost doubled in volume. Using a sharp, single-edged razor or thin-bladed knife, make three ⅛-inch-deep slashes on the top of each baguette.

Preheat the oven to 450°.

Quickly spray the inside of the oven thoroughly with a water mister. The resulting steam gives the bread a crisp crust. Bake the bread until it sounds hollow when tapped on the bottom, about 15 minutes.

WHOLE WHEAT BAGUETTES

Elite

Variation for 2 baguettes

1 cup less 1 tablespoon (7½ ounces) water
2 cups (9½ ounces) whole wheat flour
2 tablespoons gluten flour
1 teaspoon fine sea salt
1½ teaspoons active dry yeast
Cornmeal, for dusting

Put all the ingredients, except the cornmeal, in the inner pan in the order listed, or in the reverse order if the manual for your machine specifies dry ingredients first and liquids last. Select Dough setting (or the equivalent setting for your machine, see chart, pages 42–44). Push Start. When the machine beeps after 1 hour and 20 minutes, remove the dough. Turn off the machine.

Form the dough into a ball and transfer it to an oiled bowl, turning to coat the dough with oil. Cover the bowl with a damp kitchen towel or plastic wrap. Let it stand at warm room temperature for 45 to 60 minutes, until doubled in volume.

Divide the dough into 2 equal pieces. On a clean, unfloured work surface, roll and stretch each piece into an 8- to 9-inch log. Put the logs on a cornmeal-dusted baking sheet. Cover with a damp kitchen towel or plastic wrap and let stand for about 45 minutes or until almost doubled in volume. Using a sharp, single-edged razor or thin-bladed knife, make three ⅛-inch-deep slashes on the top of each baguette.

Preheat the oven to 450°.

Quickly spray the inside of the oven thoroughly with a water mister. The resulting steam gives the bread a crisp crust. Bake the bread until it sounds hollow when tapped on the bottom, about 15 minutes.

BREADS FOR HOLIDAYS AND ENTERTAINING

When the family gathers for the holidays, fill the kitchen with the comforting aromas of bread baking. Nothing welcomes them more or shows how much you care than home-baked treats. I have collected here traditional Christmas, Chanukah, and Thanksgiving breads, as well as breads that lend themselves to entertaining, whether you are planning a small, elegant dinner party or a large open-house buffet. This is the season, too, when we bake for friends and neighbors, presenting gaily wrapped loaves as tokens of good cheer and holiday wishes. Many of these breads go beyond the winter holiday season. They will become trusted companions whenever you entertain. And because you can rely on their goodness and the infallibility of the bread machine, you will be free to plan the rest of the menu with confidence.

EGG BREAD

Transition

Makes one 1½-pound loaf

Rich, tender egg breads are great favorites with a lot of folks. Since I rarely cook with whole eggs, I find liquid egg substitute does a splendid job of tenderizing and enriching the loaf.

¾ cup (6 ounces) low-fat milk
3 tablespoons canola oil
2 tablespoons honey
½ cup liquid egg substitute
3 cups (14 ounces) unbleached all-purpose flour
1½ teaspoons fine sea salt
2 teaspoons active dry yeast

Put all the ingredients in the inner pan in the order listed, or in the reverse order if the manual for your machine specifies dry ingredients first and liquids last. Select Basic Wheat cycle, Light setting (or the equivalent setting for your machine, see chart, pages 42-44). Push Start.

EGG BREAD

Transition

Variation for one 1-pound loaf

⅓ cup (2¾ ounces) low-fat milk
2 tablespoons canola oil
1½ tablespoons honey
⅓ cup plus 1 tablespoon liquid egg substitute
2 cups (9½ ounces) unbleached all-purpose flour
1 teaspoon fine sea salt
1½ teaspoons active dry yeast

Put all the ingredients in the inner pan in the order listed, or in the reverse order if the manual for your machine specifies dry ingredients first and liquids last. Select Basic Wheat cycle, Light setting (or the equivalent setting for your machine, see chart, pages 42–44). Push Start.

CHRISTMAS FRUIT BREAD

Transition

Makes one 1½-pound loaf

*C*hristmas would not seem festive without a rich spice bread generously studded with dried fruits. Be sure not to include the bitter white pith beneath the skin when grating the colorful zest from the lemons.

¾ cup (6 ounces) water
2 tablespoons canola oil
2 tablespoons maple syrup
1 large egg (or ¼ cup liquid egg substitute)
1 teaspoon vanilla extract
2¼ cups (10¾ ounces) unbleached all-purpose flour
¾ cup (3½ ounces) whole wheat flour
2 tablespoons powdered milk
Grated zest of 1½ lemons
1 teaspoon cinnamon
¼ teaspoon ground cardamom
1¼ teaspoons fine sea salt
2 teaspoons active dry yeast
¼ cup (1¼ ounces) raisins
¼ cup (1½ ounces) chopped dates
3 tablespoons chopped dried apricots
⅓ cup (½ ounce) chopped dried apples

Put all the ingredients, except the dried fruits, in the inner pan in the order listed, or in the reverse order if the manual for your machine specifies dry ingredients first and liquids last. Select Fruit & Nut setting (or the equivalent setting for your machine, see chart, pages 42–44). Push Start.

Add the dried fruits when the machine beeps, about 12 minutes after starting.

CHRISTMAS FRUIT BREAD

Transition

Variation for one 1-pound loaf

½ cup (4 ounces) water
1½ tablespoons canola oil
1½ tablespoons maple syrup
1 medium egg (or 3 tablespoons liquid egg substitute)
¾ teaspoon vanilla extract
1⅔ cups (8 ounces) unbleached all-purpose flour
⅓ cup (1½ ounces) whole wheat flour
1½ tablespoons powdered milk
Grated zest of 1 lemon
¾ teaspoon cinnamon
⅛ teaspoon ground cardamom
¾ teaspoon fine sea salt
1½ teaspoons active dry yeast
3 tablespoons raisins
3 tablespoons chopped dates
2 tablespoons chopped dried apricots
3 tablespoons chopped dried apples

Put all the ingredients, except the dried fruits, in the inner pan in the order listed, or in the reverse order if the manual for your machine specifies dry ingredients first and liquids last. Select Fruit & Nut setting (or the equivalent setting for your machine, see chart, pages 42–44). Push Start.

Add the dried fruits when the machine beeps, about 12 minutes after starting.

OVEN-BAKED CHALLAH

Transition

Makes one 1½-pound loaf

A *shiny-crusted, braided loaf of challah is a tradition in Jewish households during the holidays. The dough is easy to make in the bread machine—all that is required of you is braiding the ropes of dough to fashion the bread.*

¾ cup (6 ounces) low-fat milk
3 tablespoons canola oil
2 tablespoons honey
½ cup liquid egg substitute
3¼ cups (16 ounces) unbleached all-purpose flour
1½ teaspoons fine sea salt
2 teaspoons active dry yeast
1 egg white, lightly beaten
1 tablespoon poppy seeds

Put all the ingredients, except the egg white and poppy seeds, in the inner pan in the order listed, or in the reverse order if the manual for your machine specifies dry ingredients first and liquids last. Select Dough setting (or the equivalent setting for your machine, see chart, pages 42–44). Push Start. When the machine beeps after 1 hour and 20 minutes, remove the dough. Turn off the machine.

Divide the dough into 3 equal pieces. On a clean, unfloured work surface, roll and stretch each piece of dough into a 14-inch rope. Put the ropes on a parchment-lined baking sheet. Starting from the center and working out, braid the ropes toward one end, pinching the ends of the ropes together when finished. Repeat, working from the center, and braiding toward the opposite end. Cover the braid with a damp kitchen towel or plastic wrap and let stand at room temperature for 45 to 60 minutes, until almost doubled in volume.

Preheat the oven to 375°. Brush the top of the braid with the beaten egg white and sprinkle with poppy seeds. Bake for 35 to 45 minutes, until the bread is browned and sounds hollow when tapped on the bottom.

OVEN-BAKED CHALLAH

Transition

Variation for one 1-pound loaf

½ cup (4 ounces) low-fat milk
2 tablespoons canola oil
1½ tablespoons honey
⅓ cup plus 1 tablespoon liquid egg substitute
2¼ cups (11 ounces) unbleached all-purpose flour
1 teaspoon fine sea salt
1½ teaspoons active dry yeast
1 egg white, lightly beaten
2 teaspoons poppy seeds

Put all the ingredients, except the egg white and poppy seeds, in the inner pan in the order listed, or in the reverse order if the manual for your machine specifies dry ingredients first and liquids last. Select Dough setting (or the equivalent setting for your machine, see chart, pages 42–44). Push Start. When the machine beeps after 1 hour and 20 minutes, remove the dough. Turn off the machine.

Divide the dough into 3 equal pieces. On a clean, unfloured work surface, roll and stretch each piece of dough into a 10- to 12-inch rope. Put the ropes on a parchment-lined baking sheet. Starting from the center and working out, braid the ropes toward one end, pinching the ends of the ropes together when finished. Repeat, working from the center, and braiding toward the opposite end. Cover the braid with a damp kitchen towel or plastic wrap and let stand at room temperature for 45 to 60 minutes, until almost doubled in volume.

Preheat the oven to 375°. Brush the top of the braid with the beaten egg white and sprinkle with poppy seeds. Bake for 35 to 45 minutes, until the bread is browned and sounds hollow when tapped on the bottom.

POTATO-CHEESE SOUP BREAD

Transition

Makes one 1½-pound loaf

I rely on a good-quality dry soup mix, available at natural food stores, to give this bread its flavor and wonderful texture. It's delicious on a buffet table or for a skating, sledding, or après-ski get-together. You can experiment with flavors of soup, as well.

¾ cup (6 ounces) water
1½ tablespoons extra-virgin olive oil
1 tablespoon barley malt syrup
1 large egg (or ¼ cup liquid egg substitute)
1 package (1 ounce) potato-cheese dry soup mix
2¼ cups (10¾ ounces) unbleached all-purpose flour
¾ cup (3½ ounces) whole wheat flour
½ teaspoon fine sea salt
2 tablespoons powdered milk
2½ teaspoons active dry yeast

Put all the ingredients in the inner pan in the order listed, or in the reverse order if the manual for your machine specifies dry ingredients first and liquids last. Select Basic Wheat cycle, Medium setting (or the equivalent setting for your machine, see chart, pages 42–44). Push Start.

POTATO-CHEESE SOUP BREAD

Transition

Variation for one 1-pound loaf

½ cup (4 ounces) water
1 tablespoon extra-virgin olive oil
2 teaspoons barley malt syrup
1 medium egg (or 3 tablespoons liquid egg substitute)
¾ package (¾ ounce) potato-cheese dry soup mix
1½ cups (7½ ounces) unbleached all-purpose flour
½ cup (2½ ounces) whole wheat flour
¼ teaspoon fine sea salt
1½ tablespoons powdered milk
2 teaspoons active dry yeast

Put all the ingredients in the inner pan in the order listed, or in the reverse order if the manual for your machine specifies dry ingredients first and liquids last. Select Basic Wheat cycle, Medium setting (or the equivalent setting for your machine, see chart, pages 42–44). Push Start.

CHEDDAR AND CHIVE BREAD

Transition

Makes one 1½-pound loaf

*S*harp cheddar and mild oniony chives make this one of the best party breads I know.

⅔ cup (5½ ounces) water
2 tablespoons canola oil
1 tablespoon honey
1 cup (4 ounces) shredded extra-sharp cheddar cheese
2 large eggs (or ½ cup liquid egg substitute)
2½ cups (12 ounces) unbleached all-purpose flour
¾ cup (3½ ounces) whole wheat flour
¼ cup powdered milk
2 tablespoons dried chives
1½ teaspoons fine sea salt
2½ teaspoons active dry yeast

Put all the ingredients in the inner pan in the order listed, or in the reverse order if the manual for your machine specifies dry ingredients first and liquids last. Select Basic Wheat cycle, Light setting (or the equivalent setting for your machine, see chart, pages 42–44). Push Start.

CHEDDAR AND CHIVE BREAD

Transition

Variation for one 1-pound loaf

⅓ cup (2¾ ounces) water
1½ tablespoons canola oil
2 teaspoons honey
¾ cup (3 ounces) shredded extra-sharp cheddar cheese
2 medium eggs (or ¼ cup plus 2 tablespoons liquid egg
   substitute)
1⅔ cups (8 ounces) unbleached all-purpose flour
⅓ cup (1½ ounces) whole wheat flour
3 tablespoons powdered milk
1½ tablespoons dried chives
1 teaspoon fine sea salt
2 teaspoons active dry yeast

Put all the ingredients in the inner pan in the order listed, or in the reverse order if the manual for your machine specifies dry ingredients first and liquids last. Select Basic Wheat cycle, Light setting (or the equivalent setting for your machine, see chart, pages 42–44). Push Start.

GINGER CURRANT BREAD

Transition

Makes one 1½-pound loaf

*B*aking bread spiced with heady ginger fills the kitchen with such a comforting aroma, everyone who walks in will feel "home for the holidays."

1 cup (8 ounces) water
1½ tablespoons canola oil
2 tablespoons honey
Grated zest of 1 lemon
2½ cups (12 ounces) unbleached all-purpose flour
½ cup (2½ ounces) whole wheat flour
2 tablespoons powdered milk
1 teaspoon ground ginger
1½ teaspoons fine sea salt
2½ teaspoons active dry yeast
½ cup (2 ounces) currants

Put all the ingredients, except the currants, in the inner pan in the order listed, or in the reverse order if the manual for your machine specifies dry ingredients first and liquids last. Select Fruit & Nut setting (or the equivalent setting for your machine, see chart, pages 42–44). Push Start.

Add the currants when the machine beeps, about 12 minutes after starting.

GINGER CURRANT BREAD

Transition

Variation for one 1-pound loaf

¾ cup (6 ounces) water
1 tablespoon canola oil
1½ tablespoons honey
Grated zest of ½ lemon
1½ cups (7½ ounces) unbleached all-purpose flour
½ cup (2½ ounces) whole wheat flour
1½ tablespoons powdered milk
¾ teaspoon ground ginger
1 teaspoon fine sea salt
2 teaspoons active dry yeast
⅓ cup (1½ ounces) currants

Put all the ingredients, except the currants, in the inner pan in the order listed, or in the reverse order if the manual for your machine specifies dry ingredients first and liquids last. Select Fruit & Nut setting (or the equivalent setting for your machine, see chart, pages 42–44). Push Start.

Add the currants when the machine beeps, about 12 minutes after starting.

DINNER ROLLS

Transition

Makes 12 rolls

*H*omemade dinner rolls add a warm touch to any party. I nestle these together in the baking pan so the tops are a little crispy but the sides stay soft and tender. For more crust, leave about two inches between each one during baking.

¾ cup (6 ounces) water
1 large egg (or ¼ cup liquid egg substitute)
3 tablespoons canola oil
2 tablespoons honey
2¼ cups (10¾ ounces) unbleached all-purpose flour
¾ cup (3½ ounces) whole wheat flour
2 tablespoons powdered milk
1½ teaspoons fine sea salt
2 teaspoons active dry yeast
1 tablespoon low-fat milk
1 tablespoon poppy seeds or sesame seeds

Put all the ingredients, except the low-fat milk and poppy seeds or sesame seeds, in the inner pan in the order listed, or in the reverse order if the manual for your machine specifies dry ingredients first and liquids last. Select Dough setting (or the equivalent setting for your machine, see chart, pages 42–44). Push Start. When the machine beeps after 1 hour and 20 minutes, remove the dough. Turn off the machine.

Put the dough on a floured work surface. Gently roll and stretch it into a 12-inch rope. Slice the rope into 12 pieces and form into rolls: Put a piece of dough in your cupped palm. Cover the dough with your other, slightly cupped hand. Rotate the top hand and use your fingertips and the heel of the top hand to gently mold the dough into a ball. Repeat with the remaining dough pieces. Put the rolls in a lightly greased 10-inch square pan, leaving very little room between them. Cover the rolls with a damp kitchen towel or plastic wrap and let stand for about 45 minutes, until almost doubled in volume.

Preheat the oven to 400°. Brush the tops of the rolls with milk and sprinkle with poppy seeds or sesame seeds. Bake the rolls for 12 to 15 minutes or until lightly browned.

DINNER ROLLS

Transition

Variation for 8 rolls

½ cup (4 ounces) water
1 medium egg (or 3 tablespoons liquid egg substitute)
2 tablespoons canola oil
1½ tablespoons honey
1⅔ cups (8 ounces) unbleached all-purpose flour
⅓ cup (1½ ounces) whole wheat flour
1½ tablespoons powdered milk
1 teaspoon fine sea salt
1½ teaspoons active dry yeast
2 teaspoons low-fat milk
2 teaspoons poppy seeds or sesame seeds

Put all the ingredients, except the low-fat milk and poppy seeds or sesame seeds, in the inner pan in the order listed, or in the reverse order if the manual for your machine specifies dry ingredients first and liquids last. Select Dough setting (or the equivalent setting for your machine, see chart, pages 42–44). Push Start. When the machine beeps after 1 hour and 20 minutes, remove the dough. Turn off the machine.

Put the dough on a floured work surface. Gently roll and stretch it into an 8-inch rope. Slice the rope into 8 pieces and form into rolls: Put a piece of dough in your cupped palm. Cover the dough with your other, slightly cupped hand. Rotate the top hand and use your fingertips and the heel of your top hand to gently mold the dough into a ball. Repeat with the remaining dough pieces. Put the rolls in a lightly greased 10-inch square pan, leaving very little room between them. Cover the rolls with a damp kitchen towel or plastic wrap and let stand for about 45 minutes, until almost doubled in volume.

Preheat the oven to 400°. Brush the tops of the rolls with milk and sprinkle with poppy seeds or sesame seeds. Bake the rolls for 12 to 15 minutes or until lightly browned.

BREADSTICKS

Transition

Makes 12 breadsticks

*B*readsticks are a nice touch for a party. Prop them in pretty glasses on the table, or lay one across each guest's bread plate.

¾ cup plus 2 tablespoons (7 ounces) water
2 tablespoons extra-virgin olive oil
1 tablespoon barley malt syrup
1 large egg plus 1 egg yolk (or 5 tablespoons liquid egg
    substitute)
2½ cups (12 ounces) unbleached all-purpose flour
¾ cup (3½ ounces) whole wheat flour
2 tablespoons powdered milk
1½ teaspoons fine sea salt
2 teaspoons active dry yeast
1 egg white, lightly beaten
2 tablespoons sesame seeds or poppy seeds

Put all the ingredients, except the egg white and sesame seeds or poppy seeds, in the inner pan in the order listed, or in the reverse order if the manual for your machine specifies dry ingredients first and liquids last. Select Dough setting (or the equivalent setting for your machine, see chart, pages 42–44). Push Start. When the machine beeps after 1 hour and 20 minutes, remove the dough. Turn off the machine.

Put the dough on a lightly floured counter or board. Roll and stretch the dough into a 12-inch rope. Slice the rope into 12 pieces. Roll and stretch each piece into a thin 12-inch rope. Put the breadsticks on a baking sheet dusted with cornmeal. Lightly brush each one with egg white and sprinkle with sesame seeds or poppy seeds. Cover with a damp kitchen towel or plastic wrap and let rise for about 30 minutes, until doubled in volume.

Preheat the oven to 400°. Bake the breadsticks for 12 to 15 minutes or until golden.

BREADSTICKS

Transition

Variation for 8 breadsticks

½ cup plus 2 tablespoons (5 ounces) water
1½ tablespoons extra-virgin olive oil
2 teaspoons barley malt syrup
1 medium egg plus 1 egg yolk (or 3½ tablespoons liquid egg
  substitute)
1⅔ cups (8 ounces) unbleached all-purpose flour
⅓ cup (1½ ounces) whole wheat flour
1½ tablespoons powdered milk
1 teaspoon fine sea salt
1 teaspoon active dry yeast
1 egg white, lightly beaten
2 tablespoons sesame seeds or poppy seeds

Put all the ingredients, except the egg white and sesame seeds or poppy seeds, in the inner pan in the order listed, or in the reverse order if the manual for your machine specifies dry ingredients first and liquids last. Select Dough setting (or the equivalent setting for your machine, see chart, pages 42–44). Push Start. When the machine beeps after 1 hour and 20 minutes, remove the dough. Turn off the machine.

Put the dough on a lightly floured counter or board. Roll and stretch the dough into an 8-inch rope. Slice the rope into 8 pieces. Roll and stretch each piece into a thin 12-inch rope. Put the breadsticks on a baking sheet dusted with cornmeal. Lightly brush each one with egg white and sprinkle with sesame seeds or poppy seeds. Cover with a damp kitchen towel or plastic wrap and let rise for about 30 minutes, until doubled in volume.

Preheat the oven to 400°. Bake the breadsticks for 12 to 15 minutes or until golden.

THANKSGIVING CRANBERRY BREAD

Elite

Makes one 1½-pound loaf

*O*nce you try it, this surely will become an expected guest at your family's Thanksgiving celebrations. Many natural food stores stock cranberry sauce made with whole berries and sweetened without refined sugar. It is worth looking for.

1 cup (8 ounces) water
1½ tablespoons canola oil
1½ tablespoons honey
½ teaspoon liquid lecithin
Grated zest of 1 orange
Grated zest of 1 lemon
3 tablespoons whole cranberry sauce
3 cups (14 ounces) whole wheat flour
2 tablespoons gluten flour
3 tablespoons powdered whey
1 teaspoon fine sea salt
2½ teaspoons active dry yeast
½ cup (1½ ounces) dried cranberries

Put all the ingredients, except the dried cranberries, in the inner pan in the order listed, or in the reverse order if the manual for your machine specifies dry ingredients first and liquids last. Select Fruit & Nut setting (or the equivalent setting for your machine, see chart, pages 42–44). Push Start.

Add the cranberries when the machine beeps, about 12 minutes after starting.

THANKSGIVING CRANBERRY BREAD

Elite

Variation for one 1-pound loaf

¾ cup (6 ounces) water
1 tablespoon canola oil
1 tablespoon honey
¼ teaspoon liquid lecithin
Grated zest of ½ orange
Grated zest of ½ lemon
2 tablespoons whole cranberry sauce
2 cups (9½ ounces) whole wheat flour
1½ tablespoons gluten flour
2 tablespoons powdered whey
¾ teaspoon fine sea salt
2 teaspoons active dry yeast
⅓ cup (1 ounce) dried cranberries

Put all the ingredients, except the dried cranberries, in the inner pan in the order listed, or in the reverse order if the manual for your machine specifies dry ingredients first and liquids last. Select Fruit & Nut setting (or the equivalent setting for your machine, see chart, pages 42–44). Push Start.

Add the cranberries when the machine beeps, about 12 minutes after starting.

HAWAIIAN BREAD

Elite

Makes one 1½-pound loaf

*T*his chunky loaf tastes of the tropics at their best. Your guests will love it, and it makes a much appreciated hostess gift, too. Look for unsulfured dried fruits in the natural food store.

1 cup plus 2 tablespoons (9 ounces) water
1½ tablespoons canola oil
1½ tablespoons honey
½ teaspoon liquid lecithin
3 cups (14 ounces) whole wheat flour
3 tablespoons powdered whey
2 tablespoons gluten flour
1½ teaspoons fine sea salt
2½ teaspoons active dry yeast
1 teaspoon ground ginger
¼ cup (¾ ounce) shredded unsweetened coconut
¼ cup (1½ ounces) unsulfured, naturally sweetened dried
   pineapple, finely chopped
¼ cup (1 ounce) unsulfured dried papaya, finely chopped
¼ cup (1 ounce) chopped unsalted macadamia nuts

Put the ingredients, except the coconut, dried fruits, and nuts, in the inner pan in the order listed, or in the reverse order if the manual for your machine specifies dry ingredients first and liquids last. Select Fruit & Nut setting (or the equivalent setting for your machine, see chart, pages 42–44). Push Start.

Add the coconut, dried fruits, and nuts when the machine beeps, about 12 minutes after starting.

HAWAIIAN BREAD

Elite

Variation for one 1-pound loaf

¾ cup plus 2 tablespoons (7 ounces) water
1 tablespoon canola oil
1 tablespoon honey
¼ teaspoon liquid lecithin
2 cups (9½ ounces) whole wheat flour
2 tablespoons powdered whey
1½ tablespoons gluten flour
1 teaspoon fine sea salt
2 teaspoons active dry yeast
½ teaspoon ground ginger
3 tablespoons shredded unsweetened coconut
3 tablespoons unsulfured, naturally sweetened dried pineapple,
   finely chopped
3 tablespoons unsulfured dried papaya, finely chopped
3 tablespoons chopped unsalted macadamia nuts

Put the ingredients, except the coconut, dried fruits, and nuts, in the inner pan in the order listed, or in the reverse order if the manual for your machine specifies dry ingredients first and liquids last. Select Fruit & Nut setting (or the equivalent setting for your machine, see chart, pages 42–44). Push Start.

Add the coconut, dried fruits, and nuts when the machine beeps, about 12 minutes after starting.

ALMOND-CINNAMON ROLLS

Elite

Makes 16 rolls

*T*hese cholesterol-free cinnamon rolls will be your favorite part of a healthy, holiday brunch.

1¼ cups (10 ounces) water
2 tablespoons canola oil
2 tablespoons honey
½ teaspoon liquid lecithin
3 cups (14 ounces) whole wheat flour
4 tablespoons whey
1 tablespoon gluten flour
1 tablespoon powdered egg substitute
1 teaspoon fine sea salt
2½ teaspoons active dry yeast

Glaze

¾ cup honey
¾ cup whey
⅓ cup almond butter
⅓ cup canola oil

For sprinkling on glaze

1 tablespoon cinnamon
½ cup raisins or chopped nuts (optional)

Put all the ingredients in the inner pan in the order listed, or in the reverse order if the manual for your machine specifies dry ingredients first and liquids last. Select Dough setting (or the equivalent setting for your machine, see chart, pages 42–44). Push Start. When the machine beeps after 1 hour and 20 minutes, remove the dough. Turn off the machine.

Place the dough on a lightly floured counter or cutting board. Flatten it out slightly and roll it into a 12-by-16-inch rectangle.

Stir the glaze ingredients together until smooth. Warm gently in a saucepan for a couple of minutes if too stiff. Spread half the glaze over the rectangle of dough, leaving a narrow border all around. Sprinkle the cinnamon and, if desired, the raisins or chopped nuts over the glaze. Beginning at one long side, roll the dough into a cylinder and pinch the seam to seal. Cut the rolled dough into 1-inch slices.

Using canola oil, lightly oil a 13-by-9-inch baking pan. Spread the remaining glaze mixture over the bottom of the prepared pan. Set the rolls in the pan on top of the glaze and cover with plastic or a damp cloth. Let the rolls rise in a warm place until doubled in volume, about 1 hour.

Preheat the oven to 350°.

Set the pan on a baking sheet and bake on the center rack of the oven for 15 to 20 minutes. (Glaze that bubbles in the oven will spill onto the baking sheet.) Invert the pan onto a serving platter and let the glaze drip down the sides of the rolls. Scrape any remaining glaze from the pan onto the rolls. Serve the rolls warm.

ALMOND-CINNAMON ROLLS

Elite

Variation for 10 to 12 rolls

¾ cup plus 2 tablespoons (7 ounces) water
1½ tablespoons canola oil
1½ tablespoons honey
¼ teaspoon liquid lecithin
2 cups (9½ ounces) whole wheat flour
3 tablespoons whey
2 teaspoons gluten four
2 teaspoons powdered egg substitute
¾ teaspoon fine sea salt
1½ teaspoons active dry yeast

Glaze

½ cup honey
½ cup whey
¼ cup almond butter
¼ cup canola oil

For sprinkling on glaze

2 teaspoons cinnamon
⅓ cup raisins or chopped nuts (optional)

Put all the ingresients in the inner pan in the order listed, or in the reverse order if the manual for your machine specifies dry ingredients first and liquids last. Select Dough setting (or the equivalent setting for your machine, see chart, pages 42–44). Push Start. When the machine beeps after 1 hour and 20 minutes, remove the dough. Turn off the machine.

Place the dough on a lightly floured counter or cutting board. Flatten it out slightly and roll it into a 10-by-12-inch rectangle.

Stir the glaze ingredients together until smooth. Warm gently in a saucepan for a couple of minutes if too stiff. Spread half the glaze over the rectangle of dough, leaving a narrow border all around. Sprinkle the cinnamon and, if desired, the raisins or chopped nuts over the glaze. Beginning at one long side, roll the dough into a cylinder and pinch the seam to seal. Cut the rolled dough into twelve 1-inch slices.

Using canola oil, lightly oil a 10-inch round cake pan. Spread the remaining glaze mixture over the bottom of the prepared pan. Set the rolls in the pan on top of the glaze and cover with plastic or a damp cloth. Let the rolls rise in a warm place until doubled in volume, about 1 hour.

Preheat the oven to 350°.

Set the pan on a baking sheet and bake on the center rack of the oven for 15 to 20 minutes. (Glaze that bubbles in the oven will spill onto the baking sheet.) Invert the pan onto a serving platter and let the glaze drip down the sides of the rolls. Scrape any remaining glaze from the pan onto the rolls. Serve the rolls warm.

GOOD FRIDAY HOT CROSS BUNS

Elite

Makes 12 buns

I have always liked the tradition that calls for these sweet, soft buns on Good Friday. They are good at other times of the year, too, but be sure to give yourself a treat and make them at least once every spring.

1 cup plus 2 tablespoons (9 ounces) water
2 tablespoons canola oil
3 tablespoons maple syrup
½ teaspoon liquid lecithin
3½ cups (16¼ ounces) whole wheat flour
1 tablespoon gluten flour
1 tablespoon powdered egg substitute
3 tablespoons powdered whey
1 teaspoon cinnamon
¼ teaspoon ground cloves
¼ teaspoon grated nutmeg
Grated zest of 1½ lemons
1¼ teaspoons fine sea salt
2½ teaspoons active dry yeast
½ cup (2 ounces) currants
2 teaspoons liquid egg substitute, for glaze
2 teaspoons honey, for glaze

Put all the ingredients, except the currants, liquid egg substitute, and honey, in the inner pan in the order listed, or in the reverse order if the manual for your machine specifies dry ingredients first and liquids last. Select Dough setting (or the equivalent setting for your machine, see chart, pages 42–44). Push Start. Add the currants about 12 minutes after starting. When the machine beeps after 1 hour and 20 minutes, remove the dough. Turn off the machine.

Put the dough on a lightly floured counter or board. Lightly grease a baking pan and your hands. Shape the dough into a 12-inch log and slice the log into 12 pieces. Put 1 piece into the palm of your hand and gently shape it into a round, using the cupped fingers of the other hand.

Put the buns on the prepared pan, cover with a damp kitchen towel or plastic wrap, and let rise for about 1 hour, until doubled in volume.

Preheat the oven to 375°. Using kitchen shears, snip a cross on the top of each roll. Brush the rolls with liquid egg substitute and bake for 18 to 22 minutes, until browned.

While the buns are hot from the oven, brush with honey. Serve the rolls hot, warm, or at room temperature.

GOOD FRIDAY HOT CROSS BUNS

Elite

Variation for 8 buns

¾ cup plus 2 tablespoons (7 ounces) water
1½ tablespoons canola oil
2 tablespoons maple syrup
¼ teaspoon liquid lecithin
2¼ cups (10¾ ounces) whole wheat flour
2 teaspoons gluten flour
2 teaspoons powdered egg substitute
2 tablespoons powdered whey
¾ teaspoon cinnamon
⅛ teaspoon ground cloves
⅛ teaspoon grated nutmeg
Grated zest of 1 lemon
¾ teaspoon fine sea salt
2 teaspoons active dry yeast
⅓ cup (1½ ounces) currants
1½ teaspoons liquid egg substitute, for glaze
1½ teaspoons honey, for glaze

Put all the ingredients, except the currants, liquid egg substitute, and honey, in the inner pan in the order listed, or in the reverse order if the manual for your machine specifies dry ingredients first and liquids last. Select Dough setting (or the equivalent setting for your machine, see chart, pages 42–44). Push Start. Add the currants about 12 minutes after starting. When the machine beeps after 1 hour and 20 minutes, remove the dough. Turn off the machine.

Put the dough on a lightly floured counter or board. Lightly grease a baking pan and your hands. Shape the dough into an 8-inch log and slice the log into 8 pieces. Put 1 piece into the palm of your hand and gently shape it into a round, using the cupped fingers of the other hand. Put the buns on the prepared pan, cover with a damp kitchen towel or plastic wrap, and let rise for about 1 hour, until doubled in volume.

Preheat the oven to 375°. Using kitchen shears, snip a cross in the top of each roll. Brush the rolls with liquid egg substitute and bake for 18 to 22 minutes, until browned.

While the buns are hot from the oven, brush with honey. Serve the buns hot, warm, or at room temperature.

PUMPKIN SPICE BREAD

Elite

Makes one 1½-pound loaf

Whenever I make this bread I think of the happy winter holidays when my family gathers for lots of good meals and good times. Be sure to buy unsweetened pumpkin puree; do not attempt to make your own, as its moisture content may not be compatible with the recipe.

½ cup (4 ounces) water
1½ tablespoons canola oil
2 tablespoons unsulfured molasses
½ teaspoon liquid lecithin
1 cup (9 ounces) unsweetened canned pumpkin puree
3 cups (14 ounces) whole wheat flour
3 tablespoons powdered whey
2 tablespoons gluten flour
2 teaspoons powdered egg substitute
1 tablespoon pumpkin pie spice
1 teaspoon fine sea salt
2½ teaspoons active dry yeast
2 tablespoons hulled pumpkin seeds
⅓ cup (1½ ounces) chopped walnuts
⅓ cup (1¾ ounces) raisins

Put all the ingredients, except the pumpkin seeds, walnuts, and raisins, in the inner pan in the order listed, or in the reverse order if the manual for your machine specifies dry ingredients first and liquids last. Select Fruit & Nut setting (or the equivalent setting for your machine, see chart, pages 42–44). Push Start.

Add the pumpkin seeds, walnuts, and raisins when the machine beeps, about 12 minutes after starting.

PUMPKIN SPICE BREAD

Elite

Variation for one 1-pound loaf

⅓ cup (2¾ ounces) water
1 tablespoon canola oil
1½ tablespoons unsulfured molasses
¼ teaspoon liquid lecithin
⅔ cup (5¾ ounces) unsweetened canned pumpkin puree
2 cups (9½ ounces) whole wheat flour
2 tablespoons powdered whey
1½ tablespoons gluten flour
1½ teaspoons powdered egg substitute
2 teaspoons pumpkin pie spice
¾ teaspoon fine sea salt
2 teaspoons active dry yeast
1½ tablespoons hulled pumpkin seeds
¼ cup (1 ounce) chopped walnuts
¼ cup (1¼ ounces) raisins

Put all the ingredients, except the pumpkin seeds, walnuts, and raisins, in the inner pan in the order listed, or in the reverse order if the manual for your machine specifies dry ingredients first and liquids last. Select Fruit & Nut setting (or the equivalent setting for your machine, see chart, pages 42–44). Push Start.

Add the pumpkin seeds, walnuts, and raisins when the machine beeps, about 12 minutes after starting.

SPICED CURRANT BREAD

Elite

Makes one 1½-pound loaf

I think of nutmeg and allspice as being autumn spices, perfect for a bread meant to be served at Thanksgiving or Christmas, or during any of the parties that mark the season. This bread is a nice gift, too, for a neighbor or office mate.

1 cup (8 ounces) water
1½ tablespoons canola oil
1½ tablespoons honey
½ teaspoon liquid lecithin
3 cups (14 ounces) whole wheat flour
3 tablespoons powdered whey
2 tablespoons gluten flour
1½ teaspoons fine sea salt
1 teaspoon ground allspice
½ teaspoon grated nutmeg
2½ teaspoons active dry yeast
½ cup (2 ounces) currants

Put all the ingredients, except the currants, in the inner pan in the order listed, or in the reverse order if the manual for your machine specifies dry ingredients first and liquids last. Select Fruit & Nut setting (or the equivalent setting for your machine, see chart, pages 42–44). Push Start.

Add the currants when the machine beeps, about 12 minutes after starting.

SPICED CURRANT BREAD

Elite

Variation for one 1-pound loaf

¾ cup (6 ounces) water
1 tablespoon canola oil
1 tablespoon honey
¼ teaspoon liquid lecithin
2 cups (9½ ounces) whole wheat flour
2 tablespoons powdered whey
1½ tablespoons gluten flour
1 teaspoon fine sea salt
¾ teaspoon ground allspice
⅓ teaspoon grated nutmeg
2 teaspoons active dry yeast
⅓ cup (1½ ounces) currants

Put all the ingredients, except the currants, in the inner pan in the order listed, or in the reverse order if the manual for your machine specifies dry ingredients first and liquids last. Select Fruit & Nut setting (or the equivalent setting for your machine, see chart, pages 42–44). Push Start.

Add the currants when the machine beeps, about 12 minutes after starting.

SWEET POTATO AND RAISIN BREAD

Elite

Makes one 1½-pound loaf

*F*or the best flavor and nutrition, I recommend you take the time to bake the yams or sweet potatoes—about 1½ hours in a 350° oven—until tender. Let them cool until you can peel them, then mash and let them cool completely before making the bread.

1 cup (8 ounces) water
1½ tablespoons canola oil
1½ tablespoons unsulfured molasses
1 teaspoon vanilla extract
½ teaspoon liquid lecithin
½ cup (4½ ounces) mashed sweet potatoes or yams
3 cups (14 ounces) whole wheat flour
2 tablespoons gluten flour
3 tablespoons powdered whey
1½ teaspoons fine sea salt
2 teaspoons active dry yeast
½ cup (2½ ounces) raisins

Put all the ingredients, except the raisins, in the inner pan in the order listed, or in the reverse order if the manual for your machine specifies dry ingredients first and liquids last. Select Basic Wheat cycle, Medium setting (or the equivalent setting for your machine, see chart, pages 42–44). Push Start.

Add the raisins when the machine beeps, about 12 minutes after starting.

SWEET POTATO AND RAISIN BREAD

Elite

Variation for one 1-pound loaf

⅔ cup (5½ ounces) water
1 tablespoon canola oil
1 tablespoon unsulfured molasses
¾ teaspoon vanilla extract
¼ teaspoon liquid lecithin
⅓ cup (3½ ounces) mashed sweet potatoes or yams (see headnote on preceding page)
2 cups (9½ ounces) whole wheat flour
1½ tablespoons gluten flour
2 tablespoons powdered whey
1 teaspoon fine sea salt
1 teaspoon active dry yeast
⅓ cup (1¾ ounces) raisins

Put all the ingredients, except the raisins, in the inner pan in the order listed, or in the reverse order if the manual for your machine specifies dry ingredients first and liquids last. Select Basic Wheat cycle, Medium setting (or the equivalent setting for your machine, see chart, pages 42–44). Push Start.

Add the raisins when the machine beeps, about 12 minutes after starting.

TEA BREADS

Whether you invite friends in for an organized tea party in front of a cheerful fire or simply look forward to relaxing with a cup of hot herbal tea at the end of a busy day, these breads are the perfect accompaniment. Their sweet, rich flavors and textures provided by dried fruits and nuts make them indispensable when the kettle boils. The breads also travel well and are first-rate choices to take to a meeting or small get-together. By the same token, they are welcome house gifts or offerings for anyone with whom you want to share a bit of yourself.

BANANA WALNUT BREAD

Transition

Makes one 1½-pound loaf

The sweetness of bananas, high in potassium and so important to a healthful diet, combine with the richness of nuts in this ever popular bread.

¾ cup (6 ounces) water
1½ tablespoons walnut oil
1½ tablespoons honey
1 teaspoon vanilla extract
2 teaspoons fresh lemon juice
½ cup (4 ounces) mashed ripe banana
2½ cups (12 ounces) unbleached all-purpose flour
¾ cup (3½ ounces) whole wheat flour
2 tablespoons powdered milk
1 teaspoon fine sea salt
2½ teaspoons active dry yeast
⅓ cup (1½ ounces) chopped walnuts
⅓ cup (2 ounces) chopped dates

Put all the ingredients, except the walnuts and dates, in the inner pan in the order listed, or in the reverse order if the manual for your machine specifies dry ingredients first and liquids last. Select Fruit & Nut setting (or the equivalent setting for your machine, see chart, pages 42–44). Push Start.

Add the walnuts and dates, when the machine beeps, about 12 minutes after starting.

BANANA WALNUT BREAD

Transition

Variation for one 1-pound loaf

½ cup (4 ounces) water
1 tablespoon walnut oil
1 tablespoon honey
¾ teaspoon vanilla extract
1½ teaspoons fresh lemon juice
⅓ cup (about 3 ounces) mashed ripe banana
1⅔ cups (8 ounces) unbleached all-purpose flour
⅓ cup (1½ ounces) whole wheat flour
1½ tablespoons powdered milk
¾ teaspoon fine sea salt
2 teaspoons active dry yeast
¼ cup (1 ounce) chopped walnuts
¼ cup (1½ ounces) chopped dates

Put all the ingredients, except the walnuts and dates, in the inner pan in the order listed, or in the reverse order if the manual for your machine specifies dry ingredients first and liquids last. Select Fruit & Nut setting (or the equivalent setting for your machine, see chart, pages 42–44). Push Start.

Add the walnuts and dates when the machine beeps, about 12 minutes after starting.

ORANGE WALNUT BREAD

Transition

Makes one 1½-pound loaf

A dash or two of walnut and orange extracts intensify the fruity flavor of this moist bread, but they are not essential. High-quality extracts and fruit oils are sold in most natural food stores.

1 cup (8 ounces) water
1½ tablespoons walnut oil
1½ tablespoons honey
1 teaspoon walnut extract (optional)
½ teaspoon orange oil (optional)
½ teaspoon liquid lecithin
Grated zest of 1 orange
2½ cups (12 ounces) unbleached all-purpose flour
¾ cup (3½ ounces) whole wheat flour
2 tablespoons powdered milk
1½ teaspoons fine sea salt
1 teaspoon cinnamon
2 teaspoons active dry yeast
½ cup (2 ounces) chopped walnuts

Put all the ingredients, except the walnuts, in the inner pan in the order listed, or in the reverse order if the manual for your machine specifies dry ingredients first and liquids last. Select Fruit & Nut setting (or the equivalent setting for your machine, see chart, pages 42–44). Push Start.

Add the walnuts when the machine beeps, about 12 minutes after starting.

ORANGE WALNUT BREAD

Transition

Variation for one 1-pound loaf

¾ cup plus 2 tablespoons (7 ounces) water
1 tablespoon walnut oil
1 tablespoon honey
¾ teaspoon walnut extract (optional)
⅓ teaspoon orange oil (optional)
¼ teaspoon liquid lecithin
Grated zest of ½ orange
1¾ cups (8¾ ounces) unbleached all-purpose flour
½ cup (2½ ounces) whole wheat flour
1½ tablespoons powdered milk
1 teaspoon fine sea salt
¾ teaspoon cinnamon
1½ teaspoons active dry yeast
⅓ cup (1½ ounces) chopped walnuts

Put all the ingredients, except the walnuts, in the inner pan in the order listed, or in the reverse order if the manual for your machine specifies dry ingredients first and liquids last. Select Fruit & Nut setting (or the equivalent setting for your machine, see chart, pages 42–44). Push Start.

Add the walnuts when the machine beeps, about 12 minutes after starting.

APPLE WALNUT BREAD

Elite

Makes one 1½-pound loaf

I suggest tart, crisp Granny Smith or Pippin apples; but use whatever variety is crunchiest and seasonal in your region for this chunky bread. Try to buy unfiltered, unpasteurized apple juice for the best flavor, most nutrients, and best results.

1 cup (8 ounces) apple juice, at room temperature
1½ tablespoons walnut oil
1½ tablespoons honey
½ teaspoon liquid lecithin
Grated zest of 1 lemon
2 teaspoons fresh lemon juice
3 cups (14 ounces) whole wheat flour
¾ cup (2¼ ounces) rolled oats
3 tablespoons powdered whey
2 tablespoons gluten flour
1½ teaspoons fine sea salt
1 teaspoon cinnamon
2½ teaspoons active dry yeast
⅓ cup chopped tart apples, such as Granny Smith or Pippin
½ cup (2 ounces) chopped walnuts

Put all the ingredients, except the apples and walnuts, in the inner pan in the order listed, or in the reverse order if the manual for your machine specifies dry ingredients first and liquids last. Select Fruit & Nut setting (or the equivalent setting for your machine, see chart, pages 42–44). Push Start.

Add the apples and walnuts when the machine beeps, about 12 minutes after starting.

APPLE WALNUT BREAD

Elite

Variation for one 1-pound loaf

¾ cup (6 ounces) apple juice, at room temperature
1 tablespoon walnut oil
1 tablespoon honey
¼ teaspoon liquid lecithin
Grated zest of ½ lemon
1½ teaspoons fresh lemon juice
2 cups (9½ ounces) whole wheat flour
½ cup (1½ ounces) rolled oats
2 tablespoons powdered whey
1½ tablespoons gluten flour
1 teaspoon fine sea salt
¾ teaspoon cinnamon
2 teaspoons active dry yeast
¼ cup chopped tart apples, such as Granny Smith or Pippin
¼ cup (1 ounce) chopped walnuts

Put all the ingredients, except the apples and walnuts, in the inner pan in the order listed, or in the reverse order if the manual for your machine specifies dry ingredients first and liquids last. Select Fruit & Nut setting (or the equivalent setting for your machine, see chart, pages 42–44). Push Start.

Add the apples and walnuts when the machine beeps, about 12 minutes after starting.

WHOLE-GRAIN BANANA DATE-NUT BREAD

Elite

Makes one 1½-pound loaf

My sons cannot get enough of this classic bread. Your family surely will love it as much as mine does once it becomes part of your bread kitchen.

¾ cup plus 2 tablespoons (7 ounces) water
1½ tablespoons walnut oil
½ teaspoon liquid lecithin
1 teaspoon vanilla extract
2 teaspoons fresh lemon juice
½ cup (4 ounces) mashed ripe banana
3 cups (14 ounces) whole wheat flour
3 tablespoons powdered whey
2 tablespoons gluten flour
1 teaspoon fine sea salt
2½ teaspoons active dry yeast
⅓ cup (1½ ounces) finely chopped walnuts
⅓ cup (2 ounces) chopped pitted dates

Put all the ingredients, except the walnuts and dates, in the inner pan in the order listed, or in the reverse order if the manual for your machine specifies dry ingredients first and liquids last. Select Fruit & Nut setting (or the equivalent setting for your machine, see chart, pages 42–44). Push Start.

Add the walnuts and dates when the machine beeps, about 12 minutes after starting.

WHOLE-GRAIN BANANA DATE-NUT BREAD

Elite

Variation for one 1-pound loaf

⅔ cup (5½ ounces) water
1 tablespoon walnut oil
¼ teaspoon liquid lecithin
¾ teaspoon vanilla extract
1½ teaspoons fresh lemon juice
⅓ cup (about 3 ounces) mashed ripe banana
2 cups (9½ ounces) whole wheat flour
2 tablespoons powdered whey
1½ tablespoons gluten flour
¾ teaspoon fine sea salt
2 teaspoons active dry yeast
¼ cup (1 ounce) finely chopped walnuts
¼ cup (1½ ounces) chopped pitted dates

Put all the ingredients, except the walnuts and dates, in the inner pan in the order listed, or in the reverse order if the manual for your machine specifies dry ingredients first and liquids last. Select Fruit & Nut setting (or the equivalent setting for your machine, see chart, pages 42–44). Push Start.

   Add the walnuts and dates when the machine beeps, about 12 minutes after starting.

FRUITY ALMOND BREAD

Elite

Makes one 1½-pound loaf

Unsweetened applesauce makes this bread pleasingly moist; and both chopped and ground almonds give it crunch and bold flavor.

¾ cup plus 2 tablespoons (7 ounces) water
2 tablespoons almond butter
2 tablespoons honey
½ teaspoon liquid lecithin
1 teaspoon almond extract
½ cup (4½ ounces) unsweetened applesauce
3¼ cups (15¼ ounces) whole wheat flour
3 tablespoons powdered whey
2 tablespoons gluten flour
Grated zest of 1 orange
1 teaspoon fine sea salt
2½ teaspoons active dry yeast
½ cup (3 ounces) finely chopped unsulfured dried apricots
¼ cup (1 ounce) coarsely chopped natural almonds
¼ cup (1 ounce) ground natural almonds

Put all the ingredients, except the apricots and both kinds of almonds, in the inner pan in the order listed, or in the reverse order if the manual for your machine specifies dry ingredients first and liquids last. Select Fruit & Nut setting (or the equivalent setting for your machine, see chart, pages 42–44). Push Start.

Add the apricots and almonds when the machine beeps, about 12 minutes after starting.

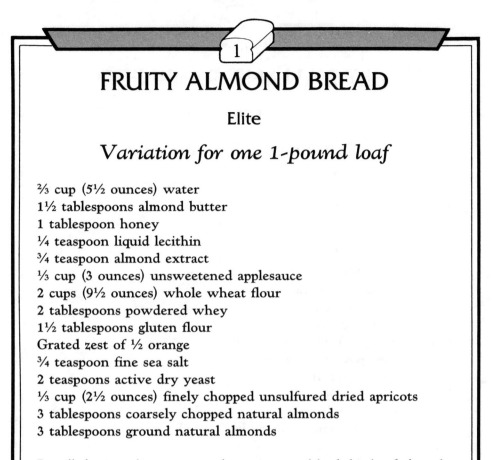

FRUITY ALMOND BREAD

Elite

Variation for one 1-pound loaf

⅔ cup (5½ ounces) water
1½ tablespoons almond butter
1 tablespoon honey
¼ teaspoon liquid lecithin
¾ teaspoon almond extract
⅓ cup (3 ounces) unsweetened applesauce
2 cups (9½ ounces) whole wheat flour
2 tablespoons powdered whey
1½ tablespoons gluten flour
Grated zest of ½ orange
¾ teaspoon fine sea salt
2 teaspoons active dry yeast
⅓ cup (2½ ounces) finely chopped unsulfured dried apricots
3 tablespoons coarsely chopped natural almonds
3 tablespoons ground natural almonds

Put all the ingredients, except the apricots and both kinds of almonds, in the inner pan in the order listed, or in the reverse order if the manual for your machine specifies dry ingredients first and liquids last. Select Fruit & Nut setting (or the equivalent setting for your machine, see chart, pages 42–44). Push Start.

Add the apricots and almonds when the machine beeps, about 12 minutes after starting.

SWEET BANANA RAISIN LOAF

Elite

Makes one 1½-pound loaf

*T*his loaf will lift your spirits at the end of a long day. Banana chips are sold loose and packaged in natural food stores and some supermarkets. Look for unsulfured chips, which are untreated and better for you. Be sure they are not sweetened—this yummy bread is sweet enough for my taste!

1 cup plus 2 tablespoons (9 ounces) water
1½ tablespoons canola oil
1½ tablespoons brown rice syrup
½ teaspoon liquid lecithin
3 cups (14 ounces) whole wheat flour
3 tablespoons powdered whey
2 tablespoons gluten flour
1½ teaspoons fine sea salt
2 teaspoons active dry yeast
½ cup (2 ounces) banana chips (dehydrated banana slices), chopped
½ cup (2½ ounces) raisins

Put all the ingredients, except the banana chips and raisins, in the inner pan in the order listed, or in the reverse order if the manual for your machine specifies dry ingredients first and liquids last. Select Fruit & Nut setting (or the equivalent setting for your machine, see chart, pages 42–44). Push Start.

Add the banana chips and raisins when the machine beeps, about 12 minutes after starting.

SWEET BANANA RAISIN LOAF

Elite

Variation for one 1-pound loaf

¾ cup (6 ounces) water
1 tablespoon canola oil
1 tablespoon brown rice syrup
¼ teaspoon liquid lecithin
2 cups (9½ ounces) whole wheat flour
2 tablespoons powdered whey
1½ tablespoons gluten flour
1 teaspoon fine sea salt
1½ teaspoons active dry yeast
⅓ cup (1½ ounces) banana chips (dehydrated banana slices), chopped
⅓ cup (1¾ ounces) raisins

Put all the ingredients, except the banana chips and raisins, in the inner pan in the order listed, or in the reverse order if the manual for your machine specifies dry ingredients first and liquids last. Select Fruit & Nut setting (or the equivalent setting for your machine, see chart, pages 42–44). Push Start.

Add the banana chips and raisins when the machine beeps, about 12 minutes after starting.

ALMOND RAISIN BREAD

Elite

Makes one 1½-pound loaf

A good measure of raisins added to this loaf complements the fine almond flavor, made all the more apparent by the addition of almond butter. Almond butter is sold in many natural food stores and specialty shops.

1 cup (8 ounces) water
1½ tablespoons almond butter
1½ tablespoons honey
½ teaspoon liquid lecithin
1 teaspoon vanilla extract
3 cups (14 ounces) whole wheat flour
3 tablespoons powdered whey
2 tablespoons gluten flour
1½ teaspoons fine sea salt
2½ teaspoons active dry yeast
½ cup (2½ ounces) raisins
½ cup (2 ounces) coarsely ground natural almonds

Put all the ingredients, except the raisins and almonds, in the inner pan in the order listed, or in the reverse order if the manual for your machine specifies dry ingredients first and liquids last. Select Fruit & Nut setting (or the equivalent setting for your machine, see chart, pages 42–44). Push Start.

Add the raisins and almonds when the machine beeps, about 12 minutes after starting.

ALMOND RAISIN BREAD

Elite

Variation for one 1-pound loaf

¾ cup (6 ounces) water
1 tablespoon almond butter
1 tablespoon honey
¼ teaspoon liquid lecithin
¾ teaspoon vanilla extract
2 cups (9½ ounces) whole wheat flour
2 tablespoons powdered whey
1½ tablespoons gluten flour
1 teaspoon fine sea salt
1½ teaspoons active dry yeast
⅓ cup (1¾ ounces) raisins
⅓ cup (1½ ounces) coarsely ground natural almonds

Put all the ingredients, except the raisins and almonds, in the inner pan in the order listed, or in the reverse order if the manual for your machine specifies dry ingredients first and liquids last. Select Fruit & Nut setting (or the equivalent setting for your machine, see chart, pages 42–44). Push Start.

Add the raisins and almonds when the machine beeps, about 12 minutes after starting.

CAROB DATE NUT BREAD

Elite

Makes one 1½-pound loaf

*S*emisweet carob chips give this bread a flavor boost hinting of chocolate. The sweet, chewy dates provide moistness and texture.

1 cup (8 ounces) water
1½ tablespoons canola oil
1½ tablespoons honey
½ teaspoon liquid lecithin
1 teaspoon vanilla extract
2 tablespoons carob powder
3 cups (14 ounces) whole wheat flour
3 tablespoons powdered whey
2 tablespoons gluten flour
1½ teaspoons fine sea salt
2½ teaspoons active dry yeast
½ cup (2 ounces) semisweet carob chips
¼ cup (1 ounce) chopped walnuts or pecans
¼ cup (1½ ounces) chopped pitted dates

Put all the ingredients, except the carob chips, nuts, and dates, in the inner pan in the order listed, or in the reverse order if the manual for your machine specifies dry ingredients first and liquids last. Select Fruit & Nut setting (or the equivalent setting for your machine, see chart, pages 42–44). Push Start.

Add the carob chips, nuts, and dates when the machine beeps, about 12 minutes after starting.

CAROB DATE NUT BREAD

Elite

Variation for one 1-pound loaf

¾ cup (6 ounces) water
1 tablespoon canola oil
1 tablespoon honey
¼ teaspoon liquid lecithin
¾ teaspoon vanilla extract
1½ tablespoons carob powder
2 cups (9½ ounces) whole wheat flour
2 tablespoons powdered whey
1½ tablespoons gluten flour
1 teaspoon fine sea salt
2 teaspoons active dry yeast
⅓ cup (1½ ounces) semisweet carob chips
3 tablespoons chopped walnuts or pecans
3 tablespoons chopped pitted dates

Put all the ingredients, except the carob chips, nuts, and dates, in the inner pan in the order listed, or in the reverse order if the manual for your machine specifies dry ingredients first and liquids last. Select Fruit & Nut setting (or the equivalent setting for your machine, see chart, pages 42–44). Push Start.

Add the carob chips, nuts, and dates when the machine beeps, about 12 minutes after starting.

BRAZIL NUT BREAD

Elite

Makes one 1½-pound loaf

Brazil nuts are especially rich and delicious in this bread, although you could substitute almonds, walnuts, pecans, or cashews, if you prefer. Brazil nuts contain selenium, a good anti-aging mineral. Also, buying Brazil nuts helps save the rain forest, where they are cultivated.

1 cup plus 2 tablespoons (9 ounces) water
1½ tablespoons walnut oil
1½ tablespoons honey
1 teaspoon vanilla extract
½ teaspoon liquid lecithin
2 teaspoons powdered egg substitute
3 cups (14 ounces) whole wheat flour
3 tablespoons powdered whey
2 tablespoons gluten flour
1½ teaspoons fine sea salt
2 teaspoons active dry yeast
½ cup (2 ounces) ground Brazil nuts
½ cup (2 ounces) chopped Brazil nuts

Put all the ingredients, except the nuts, in the inner pan in the order listed, or in the reverse order if the manual for your machine specifies dry ingredients first and liquids last. Select Fruit & Nut setting (or the equivalent setting for your machine, see chart, pages 42–44). Push Start.

Add both the ground and chopped nuts when the machine beeps, about 12 minutes after starting.

BRAZIL NUT BREAD

Elite

Variation for one 1-pound loaf

¾ cup (6 ounces) water
1 tablespoon walnut oil
1 tablespoon honey
¾ teaspoon vanilla extract
¼ teaspoon liquid lecithin
1½ teaspoons powdered egg substitute
2 cups (9½ ounces) whole wheat flour
2 tablespoons powdered whey
1½ tablespoons gluten flour
1 teaspoon fine sea salt
1½ teaspoons active dry yeast
⅓ cup (1½ ounces) ground Brazil nuts
⅓ cup (1½ ounces) chopped Brazil nuts

Put all the ingredients, except the nuts, in the inner pan in the order listed, or in the reverse order if the manual for your machine specifies dry ingredients first and liquids last. Select Fruit & Nut setting (or the equivalent setting for your machine, see chart, pages 42–44). Push Start.

Add both the ground and chopped nuts when the machine beeps, about 12 minutes after starting.

DATE AND HONEY BREAD

Elite

Makes one 1½-pound loaf

Dates and honey is an age-old combination that never loses its appeal.

1 cup (8 ounces) water
½ cup (3 ounces) chopped pitted dates
1½ tablespoons canola oil
2 tablespoons honey
½ teaspoon liquid lecithin
3 cups (14 ounces) whole wheat flour
3 tablespoons powdered whey
2 tablespoons gluten flour
1¼ teaspoons fine sea salt
2½ teaspoons active dry yeast

Put all the ingredients in the inner pan in the order listed, or in the reverse order if the manual for your machine specifies dry ingredients first and liquids last. Select Fruit & Nut setting (or the equivalent setting for your machine, see chart, pages 42–44). Push Start.

DATE AND HONEY BREAD

Elite

Variation for one 1-pound loaf

¾ cup (6 ounces) water
⅓ cup (2 ounces) chopped pitted dates
1 tablespoon canola oil
1½ tablespoons honey
¼ teaspoon liquid lecithin
2 cups (9½ ounces) whole wheat flour
2 tablespoons powdered whey
1½ tablespoons gluten flour
¾ teaspoon fine sea salt
2 teaspoons active dry yeast

Put all the ingredients in the inner pan in the order listed, or in the reverse order if the manual for your machine specifies dry ingredients first and liquids last. Select Fruit & Nut setting (or the equivalent setting for your machine, see chart, pages 42–44). Push Start.

CARROT-APPLE BREAD

Elite

Makes one 1½-pound loaf

If you own a juice extractor, chances are you make a lot of carrot-apple juice, a powerful and delicious combination. This bread puts the fiber-rich pulp to use in an equally tasty bread. Peel the carrots and apples and discard the apple seeds before juicing if you plan to use the pulp for bread. For the nuts, I suggest walnuts, pecans, or cashews.

1 cup plus 2 tablespoons (9 ounces) water
1½ tablespoons canola oil
1½ tablespoons honey
½ teaspoon liquid lecithin
¼ cup (2 ounces) carrot-apple pulp
3 cups (14 ounces) whole wheat flour
3 tablespoons powdered whey
2 tablespoons gluten flour
1 teaspoon cinnamon
1 teaspoon fine sea salt
2½ teaspoons active dry yeast
⅓ cup (1½ ounces) raisins
⅓ cup (1½ ounces) chopped walnuts

Put all the ingredients, except the raisins and nuts, in the inner pan in the order listed, or in the reverse order if the manual for your machine specifies dry ingredients first and liquids last. Select Basic Wheat cycle, Medium setting (or the equivalent setting for your machine, see chart, pages 42–44). Push Start.

Add the raisins and nuts when the machine beeps, about 12 minutes after starting.

CARROT-APPLE BREAD

Elite

Variation for one 1-pound loaf

¾ cup (6 ounces) water
1 tablespoon canola oil
1 tablespoon honey
¼ teaspoon liquid lecithin
3 tablespoons carrot-apple pulp
2 cups (9½ ounces) whole wheat flour
2 tablespoons powdered whey
1½ tablespoons gluten flour
¾ teaspoon cinnamon
¾ teaspoon fine sea salt
1½ teaspoons active dry yeast
¼ cup (1¼ ounces) raisins
¼ cup (1 ounce) chopped walnuts

Put all the ingredients, except the raisins and nuts, in the inner pan in the order listed, or in the reverse order if the manual for your machine specifies dry ingredients first and liquids last. Select Basic Wheat cycle, Medium setting (or the equivalent setting for your machine, see chart, pages 42–44). Push Start.

Add the raisins and nuts when the machine beeps, about 12 minutes after starting.

PRUNE WALNUT BREAD

Elite

Makes one 1½-pound loaf

Serve this elegant fruit bread in front of the fire with a freshly brewed pot of herb tea. The sweet flavor of the prunes shines through.

½ cup plus 2 tablespoons (5 ounces) water
1½ tablespoons walnut oil
1½ tablespoons honey
½ teaspoon liquid lecithin
½ cup (4 ounces) prune juice, at room temperature
3 cups (14 ounces) whole wheat flour
3 tablespoons powdered whey
2 tablespoons gluten flour
1½ teaspoons fine sea salt
2½ teaspoons active dry yeast
½ cup (3 ounces) chopped pitted prunes
½ cup (2 ounces) chopped walnuts

Put all the ingredients, except the prunes and walnuts, in the inner pan in the order listed, or in the reverse order if the manual for your machine specifies dry ingredients first and liquids last. Select Fruit & Nut setting (or the equivalent setting for your machine, see chart, page 42–44). Push Start.

Add the prunes and walnuts when the machine beeps, about 12 minutes after starting.

PRUNE WALNUT BREAD

Elite

Variation for one 1-pound loaf

½ cup (4 ounces) water
1 tablespoon walnut oil
1 tablespoon honey
¼ teaspoon liquid lecithin
¼ cup (2 ounces) prune juice, at room temperature
2 cups (9½ ounces) whole wheat flour
2 tablespoons powdered whey
1½ tablespoons gluten flour
1 teaspoon fine sea salt
2 teaspoons active dry yeast
⅓ cup (2½ ounces) chopped pitted prunes
⅓ cup (1½ ounces) chopped walnuts

Put all the ingredients, except the prunes and walnuts, in the inner pan in the order listed, or in the reverse order if the manual for your machine specifies dry ingredients first and liquids last. Select Fruit & Nut setting (or the equivalent setting for your machine, see chart, pages 42–44). Push Start.

Add the prunes and walnuts when the machine beeps, about 12 minutes after starting.

DATE AND FIG BREAD

Elite

Makes one 1½-pound loaf

*S*weet and sticky, figs are a most delectable fruit, and they are never better than when teamed with dates in this rich, moist, flavorful loaf.

1 cup (8 ounces) apple juice, at room temperature
1½ tablespoons canola oil
1½ tablespoons unsulfured molasses
½ teaspoon liquid lecithin
3 cups (14 ounces) whole wheat flour
3 tablespoons powdered whey
2 tablespoons gluten flour
1½ teaspoons fine sea salt
2½ teaspoons active dry yeast
⅓ cup (2 ounces) finely chopped pitted dates
⅓ cup (2½ ounces) finely chopped figs

Put all the ingredients, except the dates and figs, in the inner pan in the order listed, or in the reverse order if the manual for your machine specifies dry ingredients first and liquids last. Select Fruit & Nut setting (or the equivalent setting for your machine, see chart, pages 42–44). Push Start.

Add the dates and figs when the machine beeps, about 12 minutes after starting.

DATE AND FIG BREAD

Elite

Variation for one 1-pound loaf

⅔ cup plus 1 tablespoon (5½ ounces) apple juice, at room
temperature
1 tablespoon canola oil
1 tablespoon unsulfured molasses
¼ teaspoon liquid lecithin
2 cups (9½ ounces) whole wheat flour
2 tablespoons powdered whey
1½ tablespoons gluten flour
1 teaspoon fine sea salt
1½ teaspoons active dry yeast
¼ cup (1½ ounces) finely chopped pitted dates
¼ cup (2 ounces) finely chopped figs

Put all the ingredients, except the dates and figs, in the inner pan in the
order listed, or in the reverse order if the manual for your machine
specifies dry ingredients first and liquids last. Select Fruit & Nut setting
(or the equivalent setting for your machine, see chart, pages 42–44).
Push Start.

Add the dates and figs when the machine beeps, about 12 minutes
after starting.

SPREADS

I could not complete the book without including a sampling of natural savory and sweet spreads to top the breads. These are so good...and good for you! I have given you a few suggestions for breads that taste especially good with the individual spreads, but please, let your own tastes and preferences guide you. Serve these between two slices as sandwiches, smoothed over toast, or on small, dainty pieces of fruit and nut breads. Whatever your pleasure, rely on these and recipes of your own to help you enjoy the breads even more. A new spread makes your favorite bread new again!

GREEN OLIVE AND ROSEMARY SPREAD

Makes about 3 cups

Try this intriguing spread with Whole Wheat Baguettes (see page 192) or small, toasted pieces of Wheat Germ and Olive Oil Bread (see page 158).

1 pound imported green olives (such as Sicilian), pitted
⅓ cup pine nuts
1 clove garlic, finely chopped
Grated zest of 1 lemon
2 tablespoons fresh lemon juice
1 tablespoon chopped fresh rosemary, or 1 teaspoon dried
   rosemary
⅛ teaspoon crushed hot red pepper
½ cup extra-virgin olive oil

Soak the olives in hot water to cover for 1 hour to remove excess salt. Drain well and pat dry.

In a food processor, process the olives, pine nuts, garlic, lemon zest, lemon juice, rosemary, and red pepper until finely chopped. With the machine running, pour in the olive oil and process until the mixture is smooth.

Serve immediately or let the spread mellow for several hours in the refrigerator. It keeps, covered and refrigerated, for up to 1 week. Serve it at room temperature for the best flavor.

MEXICAN BEAN AND AVOCADO SALSA

Makes about 3 cups

This robust salsa is inspired by both classic guacamole and piquant tomato salsa. I recommend it on toasted slices of Jalapeño Corn Bread (see page 190) or between pieces of Tofu Cheese and Chive Bread (see page 186) paired with fresh alfalfa sprouts. Buy dark-skinned Haas avocados from California for the best flavor.

One 16-ounce can black beans, drained
1 ripe avocado, peeled, seeded, and chopped
1 ripe medium tomato, chopped
¼ cup chopped red onion
2 tablespoons fresh lime juice
2 cloves garlic, minced
1 fresh hot green jalapeño pepper, seeded and minced
½ teaspoon salt

Combine all the ingredients and chill for at least 1 hour before serving to allow the flavors to blend and develop. The salsa will keep, covered and refrigerated, for up to 1 day, but the sooner it is served, the better. Serve it at cool room temperature.

HERBED CUCUMBER AND YOGURT SPREAD

Makes about 2½ cups

Draining low-fat yogurt gives it a firm texture that is just right for spreads and dips. This is absolutely delicious on Finnish Rye Bread (see page 152), Caraway Onion Bread (see page 178), Pumpernickel Bread (see page 78), or any dark, flavorful bread. Kirby cucumbers are the small variety sometimes sold as ''pickling cucumbers.''

1 quart low-fat plain yogurt
3 kirby cucumbers, well scrubbed, seeds removed, finely chopped
¾ teaspoon salt
1 clove garlic, minced
1 tablespoon chopped fresh chives, or 1 teaspoon dried chives
1 tablespoon chopped fresh dill, or 1 teaspoon dried dill
1 tablespoon chopped fresh mint, or ½ teaspoon dried mint
⅛ teaspoon freshly ground pepper

Line a wire sieve with a doubled thickness of rinsed, squeezed-dry cheesecloth. Set the sieve over a bowl and spoon the yogurt into the sieve. Let the yogurt drain overnight in the refrigerator. Discard the liquid that collects in the bowl.

Toss the cucumbers with ½ teaspoon salt. Let them stand at room temperature for 1 hour to draw out excess moisture. Squeeze out excess moisture with your hands. Rinse well and pat dry.

Combine the drained yogurt with the cucumbers, garlic, chives, dill, mint, remaining ¼ teaspoon salt, and pepper. Chill for at least 1 hour to allow flavors to blend. The spread will keep, covered and refrigerated, for up to 3 days. Serve it chilled.

ROASTED ITALIAN
VEGETABLE SPREAD

Makes about 4 cups

*R*oasted summer vegetables are wonderful sandwich stuffers and also make a great pizza topping (see page 168). I suggest trying this chunky spread between generous slices of Italian Herb Bread (see page 184), Onion Thyme Bread (see page 188), or Sourdough Wheat Bread (see page 132).

1 medium eggplant (about 1 pound), cubed
2 large tomatoes, cored and quartered
3 medium zucchini, cut crosswise into ¾-inch rounds
1 large red bell pepper, stems and seeds removed, cut into
    wedges
1 medium red onion, peeled and quartered
2 tablespoons extra-virgin olive oil
¾ teaspoon salt
2 tablespoons chopped fresh basil, or 1½ teaspoons dried basil
2 cloves garlic, minced
⅛ teaspoon crushed hot red pepper

Preheat the oven to 400°.

Pierce the eggplant all over with a fork. Put it in a large baking dish with the tomatoes, zucchini, bell pepper, and onion. Drizzle with the olive oil and mix with your hands until coated. Sprinkle with the salt.

Bake for 45 to 60 minutes, until the eggplant is very soft and the vegetables are lightly browned. Toss with the basil, garlic, and hot pepper. Let the mixture cool to room temperature before serving.

GARBANZO BEAN AND CUMIN SPREAD

Makes about 3½ cups

Also known as hummus, this exotic puree has found many admirers over the last few years. You may substitute 4 cups of freshly cooked garbanzo beans—also called chick-peas—for the canned variety. Tahini (sesame seed butter) is widely available in natural food stores, specialty shops, and Asian markets. I use this as sandwich filling with sprouts and juicy, ripe tomatoes on nearly any mild-tasting bread. Try Oat Bran Bread (see page 72), High-Protein Bread (see page 86), or Honey and Flaxseed Bread (see page 182).

Two 16-ounce cans garbanzo beans, liquid reserved
½ cup sesame tahini
½ cup fresh lemon juice
3 tablespoons reserved liquid from garbanzo beans
2 cloves garlic, finely chopped
½ teaspoon ground cumin
⅛ teaspoon cayenne pepper
⅓ cup extra-virgin olive oil

Drain the garbanzo beans, reserving 3 tablespoons of the liquid. In a food processor, process the drained beans with the tahini, lemon juice, reserved bean liquid, garlic, cumin, and cayenne pepper until finely chopped. With the machine running, gradually pour in the olive oil and process until smooth. The garbanzo spread will keep, covered and re-frigerated, for 5 days. Serve it at cool room temperature.

ALMOND AND APRICOT BUTTER

Makes about 2½ cups

If you have a food processor, making nut butters is easy. You can use any sort of nut you like—the method is the same. Here, I add honey and dried apricots for sweetness and, with the fruit, chunkiness. Use it as you would peanut butter, as a sandwich filling or spread it on breakfast toast for a protein-rich start to the day. I recommend nearly any plain bread or one with almonds in it. Try Fruity Almond Bread (see page 236), English Muffin Bread (see page 104), Spelt Bread (see page 92), or Wheat Bran Bread (see page 90).

1 pound (about 4 cups) unskinned almonds
½ cup almond, walnut, or canola oil
¼ cup honey
3 tablespoons apple or prune juice
½ cup chopped unsulfured dried apricots

In a food processor, process the nuts until finely chopped. With the machine running, gradually pour in the oil, honey, and juice and process until the mixture is smooth. Add the apricots and pulse until they are finely chopped. The nut butter will keep, covered and refrigerated, for up to 1 week.

QUICK PEACH AND HONEY JAM

Makes about 1 cup

There is no pectin in this easy-to-make jam, so it will be thinner than the commercial variety. But it is so good! The recipe makes a small quantity, as the jam keeps for only a week. Spread it on breakfast toast or on tea bread for a late-day lift. Try it on Apricot Nut Bread (see page 116), toasted Sourdough Wheat Bread (see page 132), Brazil Nut Bread (see page 244), or Date and Honey Bread (see page 246).

3 ripe medium peaches (about 1 pound)
¼ cup honey
Grated zest of ½ lemon

Gently drop the peaches into a pan of boiling water and cook for 1 minute. Drain and rinse under cold water. Slip off the skins, pit the fruit, and coarsely chop it.

Combine the chopped peaches, honey, and lemon zest in a medium saucepan. Bring to a simmer and cook over medium-low heat for 10 to 15 minutes, stirring frequently, until thickened. Transfer the mixture to a blender or food processor and process until smooth. Let cool completely. The jam will keep, covered and refrigerated, for up to 1 week.

CHAPTER ·7·

MAKING BREAD BY HAND

Why, in a book celebrating the marvels of a bread machine, would I include a chapter on making bread the old-fashioned way? I have come to rely almost exclusively on the electric bread machine and I truly believe its product is as good or better than any loaf I produce by hand. But there are some persuasive arguments for baking bread a few times the way our grandmothers and great-grandmothers did nearly every week of their lives.

Notice that I say "every week" and not every day. Few homemakers, even in the days before neighborhood grocers and supermarkets, baked bread every day. It was a chore, similar to laundry and carpet beating, that was relegated to a specific day during the week. I do not doubt baking day was the most pleasant of all, but the inescapable fact is that baking bread was a necessity, a housewifely task that could not be avoided or put off for a more convenient time. The family relied on bread for sustenance. The large, homey loaves were consumed at nearly every meal and were on hand for quick snacks and late suppers. When you think about it, very few American households today are without a loaf of bread—although usually a store-bought one—for sandwiches, toast, and as an accompaniment to the evening meal. Our reliance on bread makes using the bread machine all the more important and sensible.

But I digress.

Back to making bread by hand. When you work the dough with your fingertips, you can actually feel the flour and water blending into a paste. Add the yeast, proofed and dissolved in more liquid, and the mass begins to adhere to itself and form a sticky, cohesive ball of dough. The sticky dough is ready for the fun part: kneading.

Kneading bread dough is one of the most satisfying activities known to man or woman. That may sound like hyperbole, but I urge you to try it. As you roll the dough back and forth under the heels of your hands, rhythmically pushing, folding, and gathering it, you are linked with countless generations of bread bakers who have *experienced* watching a crude mixture of flour and water, strengthened by developing gluten strands and active yeast, turn into a satiny smooth, elastic mass of dough.

When the dough is properly kneaded the real magic begins, for now is the time to leave the dough alone in a large bowl to rise. In an hour or two, the lowly lump of dough doubles in size and the tantalizing aroma of active yeast fills the kitchen, a smell rivaled only by that of baking bread.

For most breads, the risen dough must be deflated ("punched down" in bread-baking parlance), and left to rise again. It is then formed into a loaf, or loaves, put in the pan(s), and left to rise one more time. After the third rising, it is ready for baking.

WHAT DO ALL THE STEPS MEAN?

With a bread machine every step in the bread-making process is done for you, with the exception of measuring the dry and liquid ingredients. But because each step is integral to the process, it is helpful to understand them from hands-on experience.

As I explain in Chapters 3 and 4, the gluten protein in the flour develops into elastic strands when the moistened flour is manipulated and warmed. These elastic strands capture gasses emitted by dividing, fermenting yeast cells. This process raises the bread dough and ultimately gives the baked loaf its characteristic light texture.

Mixing the dough is the first step. If the dough feels dry and crumbly in the bowl, add a little more water (or other liquid such as juice). If the dough is excessively wet or runny, add more flour. When the time is right for turning it out of the mixing bowl and onto the breadboard for kneading, the dough should be damp, sticky, and cohesive. You will learn to sense the correct consistency after a few loaves.

Kneading the dough is one of the most crucial steps. The heat caused by the friction of movement initiates the development of the gluten and also helps the yeast along. When the gluten is nicely developed, the dough is ready for rising. This point is determined by a smooth feeling piece of kneaded dough that is obviously stretchy, plump, and, when poked, springs back. To knead, firmly push the dough back and forth on a lightly floured surface with the heels of your hands, folding it back on itself and smoothing it out again. For a single loaf of bread, kneading takes from eight to ten minutes, maybe a little longer. For two loaves, kneading takes close to fifteen minutes. But once you get the hang of it, the exercise is relaxing in its rhythmic motion.

Proper rising requires a warm, draft-free environment and plenty of time. During rising, the yeast cells ferment, or multiply, and the gluten strands continue to expand with captured gases. This lifts the dough to light, airy heights that will be duplicated, finally, in the oven. If you mistakenly leave the bowl near an open window or in a cold pantry, the gluten will not develop very satisfactorily nor will the dough rise as high as it should. The baked bread will be heavy and dense—the results, also, of not *enough* rising time.

Many recipes suggest rubbing the bowl used for rising with oil or butter and then rolling the mass of kneaded dough over the surface to coat it with the fat and keep the dough from drying out. But whether you take this precaution or not, do not leave the rising dough for longer than needed for the mass to double. Overisen dough may yield a loaf with a yeasty flavor, an uneven or dense crumb, and possibly a cracked, lifted, or blistered crust.

The second rising accomplishes the same end as the first. Punching down the dough expels excess gas and, with the second rising—which takes nearly as long as the first rising—the yeast and gluten interact all over again. This makes the bread's structure stronger and firmer. For the third rising, you usually form the dough into a loaf and let it rise in the bread pan. When properly risen, again doubled in size for most recipes, the bread is ready to bake in a preheated oven. The heat of the oven will cause fast rising—until the internal temperature of the loaf reaches about 120° and the yeast dies. From that point onward, the bread simply bakes and sets.

Baked bread sounds hollow on the bottom when tapped. Tapping the top crust gives you a good indication, too, but it is best to turn the loaf out of the pan and test the bottom. Look at the bread after the first time check provided by the recipe. Your eye will tell you a lot, too.

As tempting as it is to cut into hot bread, try to control the impulse. Cooled bread slices much better than warm bread and its final texture is better, too. Let the bread cool on a rack so that air circulates all around it. If you leave it sitting in the pan, the bottom may turn soggy. This holds for bread baked in the bread machine, too. Do not leave it in the pan for very long after baking. Remove it and let it cool on a rack.

Store the baked bread, whether made by hand or in the bread machine, in a cool, dry place. Pop it in a paper sack or wrap it in a clean dish towel and tuck it in a bread box, or, for longer storage, put it in a plastic bag and keep it in the refrigerator. Baked (and completely cooled) bread freezes very nicely when wrapped in plastic wrap and then foil. Date the loaves and consume them within a month or two. Let the bread thaw at room temperature before slicing it.

THE ADVANTAGES AND DISADVANTAGES OF MAKING BREAD BY HAND

I think it is a good idea to make bread by hand every now and again. Even the most experienced bakers learn from each loaf, and the lessons for neophytes are invaluable. What is more, making bread by hand nourishes the soul just as the bread feeds the body.

Making bread this way takes time and patience. It also requires judgment, and the possibility of failure lurks not far from every attempt—particularly when you are just starting out. Nevertheless, bread baking is not terribly difficult, and you will feel justly proud of the nobly browned loaves you pull from the oven.

You cannot rush bread. The gluten needs time to develop, both during kneading and then during rising. There are no shortcuts, and if you do not have the hours, there is no point beginning a recipe. Wait for a day when you have the time, when the kitchen is nice and warm, and you feel like nurturing yourself and your family in a very special way. If you must, you can retard the gluten development for four or five hours by putting the kneaded dough in the refrigerator. Let it come to room temperature and then rise as indicated in the recipe. But this is not an ideal solution and will not result in the best bread you can make.

The ever-present question of time is one of the best arguments I have for using a bread machine. All you need to do is measure the dry and liquid ingredients, put them in the machine, and then flip the switch. The machine does the rest. When you walk in the door after work, running errands, or playing volleyball, you will be greeted with the aroma of freshly baked bread. I guarantee, once you have tried a few loaves by hand, you will appreciate even more how miraculous the bread machine actually is!

CHAPTER
·8·

A GLOSSARY
OF INGREDIENTS

The most important ingredient in any bread recipe is the flour. My recipes, which call mostly for whole-grain flours, are designed to be especially healthful, hearty, and tasty. But as wholesome as the flour may be, other ingredients—from dried fruits to powdered whey—play a vital role. They add flavor, texture, color, and a high level of nutrition not found in any other breads—those you make yourself or those you buy from bakeries.

Because some of the ingredients I require may be unfamiliar, I have listed them here to explain what they are, how I use them and, perhaps most important, where you can buy them. I have also included storing information when appropriate, for what good is a block of nutritious tofu or a handful of granola if it is spoiled from incorrect storage?

You will find that nearly all these products are sold in natural food stores, although many are also sold in ordinary supermarkets, co-ops, progressive supermarkets, and specialty stores. I urge you to get to know the local natural or health food store. The people who work there are usually knowledgeable and friendly, ready to answer your questions, and suggest ingredients you may not have previously considered. These small markets are frequently good places to buy organic produce, fresh whole wheat pasta, fresh juices, and home-baked breads (although with a bread machine, that last consideration is moot!). They also may stock books on natural healing and vegetarian cooking, and some have lunch bars where you can buy delicious sandwiches, nutritious soups, and lovely, fresh salads. I find that most natural food stores are reminiscent of the old-fashioned corner grocery: The owners are friendly and know both the customers and the stock. They are eager to talk to the former about the latter whenever the need arises.

The best breads are made from the best ingredients. Once you find a good source for whole-grain flours, take a look around and seek out the best in the other ingredients. I hope the following glossary will answer a lot of your questions and pique your interest in investigating some of the marvelous and healthful products on the market today.

Ascorbic acid is also known as vitamin C and, when added to bread dough, conditions it for soft texture and helps the bread stay moist a little longer than usual. I have not included it in any of the recipes, but if you would like to try it, crush one 100-milligram tablet between two spoons and put the powder in the pan with the liquid ingredients. I use it often when I make bread for a soft, silky textured loaf.

Banana chips are dried banana slices that often are dipped in honey or sugar for sweetness and as a preservative. They also are sold unsweetened, which is the kind I use in my recipes. Some supermarkets carry banana chips, but the best source is natural food stores where they are sold in bulk. They also are available packaged. Store banana chips in a lidded jar or canister to preserve dryness.

Bran is the outer layer of the grain. It is a good source of fiber and as such may be insoluble or soluble (see Chapter 2 on page 11 for a discussion of fiber). Oat bran is primarily soluble, while wheat bran is insoluble. Bran contains some B vitamins. Praised for its contribution to colon health and to helping maintain healthy levels of cholesterol in the blood, bran has its limits. Too much fiber can interfere with the absorption of certain minerals and may even contribute to irritation in the colon. For the best balance of nutrients, bran should be left intact with the grain from which it originated, as it is in whole-grain flours. Store bran in a dry place in an airtight container.

Carob chips are an alternative to chocolate chips in baking and snacking. They are caffeine-free, which may make them a more healthful choice, but carob chips are considered a high-fat food and are usually manufactured with partially hydrogenated oils. Be sure to buy fruit-sweetened semisweet carob chips, not unsweetened.

Carob powder is a chocolate-colored powder ground from the seed pods of a Mediterranean evergreen tree. It is used most commonly as an alternative to cocoa powder and chocolate, both of which are naturally bitter and therefore need sweetening to make them palatable. Carob has a natural sweetness and does not need a lot of added sugar. The low-fat powder can be used in baking and beverage recipes, and sprinkled on desserts.

Dried beans are a great, inexpensive source of protein and calcium. Abundant variety is available including pintos, turtles, great white Northern, cranberry, fava, and garbanzo, to name only a few. Dried beans need to be soaked in cold water for about eight hours to break them down and make them digestible. Once soaked, they should be drained and then cooked in fresh water; cooking time varies between one and a half to three hours. Store dry beans in a cool, dry place. They keep for months.

Dried fruits are dehydrated sliced or whole fruits meant to be eaten on their own as sweet snacks or in trail mixes and as additions to cereals. They are also very often added to baked goods, such as bread. Raisins are perhaps the most familiar dried fruit, although apricots and dates are popular as well. Some manufacturers add sulfur dioxide to preserve the color of the fruit, while others treat it with potassium sorbate to combat fungus and mold. Unsulfured dried fruits are preferred and can be found in natural food stores and some specialty markets. The law requires that this information appear on the label. Unsulfured dried fruits are often available pesticide-free as well. Dates should be refrigerated, but store other dried fruit in covered containers at room temperature.

Egg substitute is used to avoid cholesterol and many people use it as the main component of egg dishes. Artificial eggs, egg substitutes, and egg replacers are available in powder and liquid forms. Products manufactured to replace eggs may contain egg white, oil, and milk or soy. I rely on both powdered egg substitute and liquid egg substitute in my recipes, using the powdered egg substitute mostly in the elite recipes. It contains no animal products and lightens and leavens the loaves just as eggs do. Look for powdered egg substitute in natural food stores. Liquid egg substitutes are sold in cartons in the refrigerator section of supermarkets. A scant ¼ cup of liquid egg substitute is equal to a large egg; 4 tablespoons are equal to a large egg. It is also good for brushing on hand-formed loaves as a glaze. Liquid egg substitute should be stored in the refrigerator and used by the date indicated on the package. Dry egg substitutes can be stored on the pantry shelf.

Extracts are liquid flavorings that commonly are made by blending an oily essence of a flavor (such as orange, cinnamon, vanilla, etc.) with alcohol. Choose only natural, not imitation extracts. These are sold in natural food stores in small bottles and should be stored in a cool, dry cupboard with the caps firmly screwed in place to prevent evaporation.

Granola is a dry cereal made from rolled grains (oats, wheat, rye, and barley), dried fruit, nuts and seeds. It was conceived by the Swiss as a healthful food, providing nourishment at alpine heights. The mixture is usually sweetened with honey or maple syrup, mixed with a little vegetable oil, and then roasted. As delicious as this sounds—and many granolas are glorious—granolas can be high in fat and calories and so should be used judiciously. Granola is eaten as a snack and a breakfast cereal, and handfuls may be baked into breads for crunch and sweet flavor. Read the ingredients on the package carefully to determine the fat and calorie count and to decide if a particular mixture will complement your recipe or appetite. Store most granola as you do breakfast cereal, or keep it refrigerated because of the oils in the nuts and grain.

Herbs and spices can be used fresh or dried to enhance the flavor of foods. Many contain valuable vitamins and minerals and for years have been touted as having healing powers.

Dried herbs are available all year long in supermarkets, groceries, specialty stores, and natural food stores. Although many manufacturers sell them in small plastic containers, they do best in glass. Store the herbs and spices in a dry, cool cupboard and date the bottles and jars. Replace dried leaf herbs and ground spices, such as ginger and cinnamon, every three to four months. Whole spices such as cardamom seeds and nutmeg will keep for ten to twelve months.

Dried herbs can be substituted for fresh by using a third as much as called for in a recipe. For example, a tablespoon of a fresh herb should be replaced with a teaspoon of a dried herb. Many of the breads in the book call for dried herbs and please use them, rather than fresh, whenever listed. Their flavor is more intense and generally they perform better in the bread machine.

Juices are the extracted liquid from fruits and vegetables. Juice is a delicious, nutritious beverage, as well as a natural sweetener for dressings, sauces, desserts and cereals. Drink the juice for its nutritive benefits, and if you want to experiment adding juice to bread, be sure it is at room temperature when you use it.

Fresh juices can be made at home with a juice extractor. By using this method, they retain the maximum number of nutrients possible and supply the body with concentrated vitamins and minerals—and they taste great, too. Freshly squeezed orange and grapefruit juice contain pulp. Citrus juice extracted from a juicer is pulp-free.

Juices can also be purchased from a natural food store or grocery but some nutrient loss inevitably occurs as they sit on the shelf. If you don't have a juice extractor, buy unpasteurized apple juice and freshly made carrot juice from a natural food store rather than pasteurized, crystal-clear apple juice and orange juice in a carton from the supermarket. During the fall, orchards sell freshly made apple cider, which is the same thing as unpasteurized apple juice. This is tasty and healthful and if refrigerated will keep for four or five days. Freshly made carrot juice should be consumed as soon after it is made as possible, preferably the same day.

Juice pulp is the fibrous portion of fruits and vegetables extracted during juicing. Juice pulp can be used in baking cakes, pies, muffins, and breads. Vegetable pulp works well in soups and sauces as well as some breads. Other uses of pulp include mixing with pet food as a fiber supplement, composting, and even creating your own facial—carrot/ apple pulp makes a refreshing mask. Juice pulp is nearly impossible to buy, but with a juicer, you will have an almost endless supply. It does not keep for more than a few hours at the most, although it can be frozen for later use.

Lecithin is a member of the phospholipid family and is manufactured and used by the body to help emulsify cholesterol and fats for easier utilization. Because lecithin helps break up fats and thereby prevents them from quick spoiling, it often is added to food as a natural preservative. I add it to bread doughs to condition them. Lecithin helps the gluten develop and therefore aids in the rising process and makes a big difference in the final texture and flavor of the bread.

Lecithin is found abundantly in soy foods and vegetable oils. For the recipes calling for lecithin, use liquid lecithin, readily available in natural food stores, or lecithin granules. The measurements are the same: A tablespoon of liquid lecithin is equal to a tablespoon of granules. The liquid is less expensive but very sticky; the granules are easier to use but may be a little harder to find. Buy it in large jars and store it at room temperature. I find keeping liquid lecithin in a plastic squeeze bottle makes it easy to use. One slight squeeze to the count of two produces about a half teaspoon of lecithin. I use plastic squeeze bottles for vegetable oil and honey, too.

9-grain cereal meal is a hot breakfast cereal that combines rice, wheat, oats, millet, flax, rye, barley, and a variety of other grains to create a smooth, creamy, satisfying dish. I also add it to bread for a megadose of healthful grains and a slightly crunchy texture. There are also 7- and 4-grain cereal meals.

Nuts and seeds are the edible kernel found inside a hard, removable shell. A powerhouse of nutrients, these versatile foods contain ample quantities of protein, oils, vitamins, and minerals. They are also high in fat. Because of the oil, nuts and seeds spoil quickly and should be stored in the refrigerator or freezer in a tightly sealed container.

Whenever possible, buy nuts in the shell and shell them yourself. This ensures freshness, although for amounts required for baking this can be a tedious task. The next best thing is to buy whole nutmeats, not broken pieces, which may be older and, therefore, closer to spoiling. Buy nuts from a natural food or specialty store with a good turnover, which ensures freshness. Be sure the nuts you buy are not salted or flavored, unless the recipe specifies they should be.

Nut and seed butters are finely or coarsely ground nuts or seeds used as a spread or added to recipes to create sauces, dips, dressings, and loaves of bread. The most common nut butter is the all-American peanut butter, but sesame paste (tahini) and walnut and pecan butter are available, too. You can make your own nut butters in a food processor or blender, although they will not be as smooth as commercially processed butters. Natural food stores sell unsweetened peanut butter, made fresh daily or several times a week, which is a better choice than the jars sold in supermarkets. If you buy peanut butter in a grocery store, read the label for added ingredients—do not be misled by the word "natural" in the name. Many contain sugar or hydrogenated oils. And even those made without sugar are naturally high in calories and fat. Exotic or homemade nut and seed butters and pastes should be refrigerated. They separate from their oil and so you should stir them before using.

Oils are derived from any number of seeds and vegetables. Some of the most common are corn oil, soybean oil, safflower seed oil, olive oil, peanut oil, and canola oil. I prefer *expeller pressed* oils, which are cool pressed and extracted with little or no solvent. They are, I believe, more nutritious than those extracted by solvents and heat. Unrefined oils are easy to spot as they usually are dark in color and may have sediment at the bottom of the bottle. Buy oils that are sold in glass bottles. Unlike their more highly processed cousins, unrefined oils have a relatively short shelf life.

Undoubtedly you have heard a lot about saturated, monounsaturated, and polyunsaturated fats (and oils, which are a type of fat). These terms sound intimidating but in fact are simple to understand. Whether a fat is saturated or not has to do with its chains of hydrocarbons and how they are bonded. What we need to grasp is that saturated fats, derived mostly from animal products, appear to raise levels of serum cholesterol in the blood, which is not healthy. Unsaturated fats, both monounsaturated and polyunsaturated, help lower total cholesterol in the blood, which is good! All oils are composed of proportions of poly-, mono-, and saturated fats. But some have far more of the qualities of one than the other. Some oils are made so that they are high oleic. This means their molecules have a high percentage of double hydrocarbon bonds, which are unsaturated. High-oleic oils are primarily monounsaturated.

Polyunsaturated fats apparently lower HDL levels (''good'' cholesterol) *and* LDL levels (''bad'' cholesterol), making no differentiation between the two. Monounsaturated fats lower only LDL cholesterol levels and leave HDL cholesterol alone.

If you are still confused, remember this: Oils that are primarily monounsaturated are preferred—canola, high-oleic safflower and sunflower, olive, and peanut oils are monounsaturated. Polyunsaturated oils are a close second—corn, soybean, and regular safflower and sunflower oil. Saturated fats should be avoided—butter, lard, tropical oils, such as coconut and palm oil, and shortening or hydrogenated or partially hydrogenated oils. Hydrogenation and partial hydrogenation, the process that turns vegetable oil into solid vegetable shortening (such as Crisco), makes oils more saturated than they are otherwise. Many commercial bread makers use hydrogenated oil to make the bread taste moist. Be sure to read the label and avoid it whenever possible.

I will not attempt to describe every type of oil but the following are four of my favorites and those I consider the best for you. Too much oil is not good for anyone—it's high in calories and fat—but a little is essential for everyone. Store oils in tightly capped, dark, glass bottles, if possible, in a cool, dark cupboard. Depending on the type, oils turn rancid quickly if improperly stored but otherwise keep for four or five months. Some turn cloudy when refrigerated, but do keep a few months longer. Let them stand at room temperature to liquify before using.

Canola oil is very lightly colored and almost without flavor. A primarily monounsaturated oil and an excellent source of omega-3 fatty acids, its high smoking point makes it good for cooking. I use it frequently in baking. There is no "canola" grain—the oil derives its name from Canada, its country of origin, where a variety of rapeseed was cultivated specifically for this healthful oil.

High-oleic oils are made from a hybrid seed and top canola oil when it comes to monounsaturated properties. If you cannot find canola oil, use these. They are easily available in natural food stores and progressive supermarkets.

Olive oil is unmistakably fruity in flavor and adds a special touch to many dishes and salad dressings. It is the only oil that is actually cold-pressed. It is primarily monounsaturated and the best high-oleic oil money can buy. This contributes to its poor cooking qualities (it breaks down at high temperatures), although for many baking needs I find it superb.

You have heard of extra-virgin, virgin, and pure olive oils. These simply refer to the grade of oil, with the extra-virgin coming from the first, most flavorful pressing and pure olive oil from later pressings. Extra-virgin and virgin tend to taste fruitier and look greener than pure olive oil. Use these in salad dressings more than frying.

Safflower oil is a versatile, mild-flavored product ranging in color from pale to amber. The darker the oil, the nuttier the taste, but even the darkest safflower oil is noticeably bland. High-oleic safflower oil, which is primarily monounsaturated, is appropriate for many baking needs as well as for light sautéing and in salad dressings requiring no heat at all. Both types are available in natural food stores and progressive supermarkets.

Sea salt is made from saltwater and although it is predominantly sodium chloride, it frequently contains trace minerals such as magnesium, calcium, and potassium. Sea salt is sold in supermarkets, groceries, and natural food stores, both finely and coarsely ground. For my recipes, I use finely ground sea salt.

Sweeteners can be chosen from among numerous alternatives to sugar. Some you can buy nearly anywhere, others are most easily found in natural food stores. Refined white sugar may be the sweetener of choice of most Americans, but I try very hard to avoid it. It provides empty calories with no nutritional value. Brown sugar, which is simply processed slightly differently, is no better. Both promote tooth decay and will not benefit your health in any way. Honey and syrups are just as sweet or sweeter and contribute fresh flavor and at least a few nutrients. I use these alternative sweeteners in my recipes and while they all taste different from one another, they are interchangeable in the recipes.

Barley malt is a thick, syrupy sweetener made from barley. Because it contains some complex carbohydrates and its sugar is mainly maltose and a little glucose (not sucrose or fructose), it is gentler on the system and metabolizes more easily than other sweeteners. It is dark and thick, tastes a little like molasses, with a similar burnt flavor, and adds distinctive flavor to breads and other baked goods. Take care not to use diastatic malt in the recipes; it is far too sweet for the yeast.

Honey is considered the original sweetener. Surely everyone recognizes the biblical reference to the land of "milk and honey." Its flavor and color vary depending on the flowers from which the nectar was gathered. Clover honey is most common, but you can also buy orange-blossom honey, blueberry honey, raspberry honey, and so on. Honey is nearly twice as sweet as sugar, so use less when substituting it in a recipe.

Maple syrup is a pleasantly sweet product made from the boiled sap of maple trees. Maple syrup varies from golden brown to dark amber and as the grades darken, the flavor intensifies subtly. The syrup is made in the late winter and early spring when the sap runs most freely. It takes forty gallons of sap to produce one gallon of syrup, which explains, in part, why pure maple syrup is expensive. Maple products are also available in dry crystals and a soft spread. Be sure to buy *pure* maple syrup, not maple-flavored corn or sugar syrup. The difference in flavor, texture, and goodness is the difference between a stand of stately Vermont maple trees and a polluting processing plant in a grimy city. Maple syrup is sold in specialty shops and supermarkets. For the freshest quality, buy it from a farmer who makes it himself.

Molasses is the liquid produced from the juice of sugar cane during white sugar refining. During processing, several grades of molasses emerge, with blackstrap being the most concentrated, bitter, burnt tasting, and nutritious. Look for the words "unsulfured molasses" on the label. Unsulfured molasses is available in natural food stores, specialty shops, and some supermarkets.

Rice syrup is a mild-tasting syrup derived from fermented sweet rice. I use this versatile sweetener often in bread recipes as its mildness blends well with the whole grains and other ingredients. The syrup is easy on the digestive system, not unlike barley malt. In fact, rice syrup is also called "rice malt." It should contain no fructose or sucrose. Buy rice syrup in natural food stores, where it usually is labeled as brown rice syrup.

Sucanat is the brand name for granulated, evaporated organic cane juice. The sweetener undergoes none of the bleaching or chemical treatment most cane does when it is refined for white and brown sugar. It also contains the valuable minerals present in the cane plant, all of which are lost during refining. Sucanat is sold in most natural food stores.

Tofu is a popular, versatile food made from cultured soybeans. It is sold in many supermarkets, greengrocers, Asian markets, natural food stores, and specialty shops. While tofu is most often found in the refrigerator section of the grocery, some Asian markets sell blocks of off-white tofu from water-filled trays nestled in with the produce. The firmer the tofu, the more concentrated the nutrients—and tofu, brimming with valuable vitamins and minerals, is a terrific source of protein. It is also low in fat and sodium. Firm and extra-firm tofu cakes are best for stir-frying and sautéing; soft, silken tofu resembles soft, young cheese and works well in dips, spreads, salad dressings, and desserts. Although it can be used in place of cheese in some recipes, tofu does not melt. Keep tofu covered with water, in the refrigerator. Change the water every day to keep the soybean cake fresh for up to a week.

Tofu cheese is a different product from tofu. It is often flavored like cheese and can be used in place of it. Look for it in natural food stores.

Whey is the watery part of milk remaining after casein, its principal protein, is removed. Whey may be used as an additive to recipes in place of milk but it is *not* lactose-free. I use it in many of the bread recipes because it conditions the dough so that the final texture of the bread is firm but never hard or too chewy. Buy powdered whey in jars in natural food stores and store it in a cool, dry cupboard.

Zest is the colorful outermost part of the rind of a citrus fruit. Make sure not to include the bitter white pith in recipes that call for zest.

FURTHER READING

Brody, Jane. *Jane Brody's Good Food Book.* New York: W. W. Norton & Company, Inc., 1985.

East West Journal, the Editors of. *Shopper's Guide to Natural Foods.* Garden City, New York: Avery Publishing Group, Inc., 1987.

Kordich, Jay. *The Juiceman's Power of Juicing.* New York: William Morrow and Company, 1992.

Leonard, Thom. *The Bread Book: A Natural, Whole-Grain Seed-To-Loaf Approach to Real Bread.* Brookline, Massachusetts: East West Health Books, 1990.

McGee, Harold. *On Food and Cooking.* New York: Charles Scribner's Sons, 1984.

University of California, Berkeley, the editors of "The Wellness Letter." *The Wellness Encyclopedia.* Boston: Houghton Mifflin Company, 1991.

Van Meer, Joyce. *Grains.* Louisville, Kentucky: IACP Research Report, October, 1987.

Zaret, Barry L., M.D., Marvin Moser, M.D., and Lawrence S. Cohen, M.D. *Yale University School of Medicine Heart Book.* New York: Hearst Books, 1992.

Index

wholesome multi-grain bread (elite), 80, 81

Challah, oven-baked (transition), 198, 199

Chamomile bread (elite), 94, 95

Cheddar cheese:
    bread (transition), 124, 125
    and chive bread (transition), 202, 203

Cheese:
    cheddar and chive bread (transition), 202, 203
    cheddar bread (transition), 124, 125
    cottage, and herb bread (transition), 164, 165
    -potato soup bread (transition), 200, 201

Cheese, tofu, 274
    and chive bread (elite), 186, 187

Chick-pea, see Garbanzo bean

Children, health of, 3

Chive:
    and cheddar bread (transition), 202, 203
    and tofu cheese bread (elite), 186, 187

Cholesterol, 10, 11, 266, 267, 271

Christmas fruit bread (transition), 196, 197

Cinnamon:
    almond rolls (elite), 214–215, 216–217
    honey rolls (transition), 96–97, 98–99

Cooling bread, 263–264

Corn, 17, 25
    health benefits of, 22

Cornmeal, 25
    bagels (transition), 100–101, 102–103
    herb bread (elite), 180, 181
    jalapeño bread (elite), 190, 191
    pilgrim bread (elite), 160, 161

Cottage cheese:
    cheddar cheese bread (transition), 124, 125
    and herb bread (transition), 164, 165

Cranberry bread, Thanksgiving (elite), 210, 211

Croutons, Italian herb, 184

Crunchy sunflower and millet bread (elite), 154, 155

Cucumber and yogurt spread, herbed, 256

Cumin and garbanzo bean spread, 258

Currant:
    bread, spiced (elite), 224, 225
    ginger bread (transition), 204, 205

Dairy products, 12, 13

Date(s):
    banana walnut bread (transition), 228–229
    carob nut bread (elite), 242, 243
    Christmas fruit bread (transition), 196, 197
    and fig bread (elite), 252, 253
    fruit and bran muffin bread (elite), 118, 119
    and honey bread (elite), 246, 247
    -nut banana bread, whole-grain (elite), 234, 235

Diet, changing of, 12–13

Dill rye bread (elite), 144, 145

Dinner rolls (transition), 206, 207

Dough:
    kneading of, in Breadman, 47
    making of, in Breadman, 47

Easy onion bread (transition), 126, 127

Easy pizza sauce with sweet red pepper and olive topping, 168

Egg bread (transition), 194–195

Egg replacer, 267

Elite breads, 4, 50, 53–54
    almond-cinnamon rolls, 214–215, 216–217
    almond raisin, 240, 241
    amaranth soy, 88, 89
    apple walnut, 232, 233
    apricot nut, 116, 117
    Brazil nut, 244, 245
    buckwheat oat, 82, 83
    caraway onion, 178, 179
    carob date nut, 242, 243
    carrot-apple, 248, 249
    chamomile, 94, 95
    cornmeal herb, 180, 181
    crunchy sunflower and millet, 154, 155
    date and fig, 252, 253
    date and honey, 246, 247
    dill rye, 144, 145
    Finnish rye, 152, 153

Maple syrup, 273
  pecan bread (elite), 120, 121
Mexican bean and avocado salsa, 255
Millet, 26
  health benefits of, 23
  sprouted seven seed bread (elite), 74,
    75
  and sunflower bread, crunchy (elite),
    154, 155
Milling, of flour, 15–16, 18–19, 20
  at home, 20–21
Minerals, 22–23, 266
Molasses, 273
Muffin bread, fruit and bran (elite), 118,
  119
Multi-grain cereal, 270
  bread (transition), 62, 63
  rolled grains bread (elite), 64, 65
  wholesome bread (elite), 80, 81

Natural food stores, 265–266
9-grain cereal mix, 270
Nut(s), 270
  almond and apricot butter, 259
  almond-cinnamon rolls (elite), 214–215,
    216–217
  almond raisin bread (elite), 240, 241
  apple walnut bread (elite), 232, 233
  apricot bread (elite), 116, 117
  banana walnut bread (transition), 228–
    229
  Brazil, bread (elite), 244, 245
  carob date bread (elite), 242, 243
  carrot-apple bread (elite), 248, 249
  date banana bread, whole-grain (elite),
    234, 235
  fruit and bran muffin bread (elite), 118,
    119
  fruity almond bread (elite), 236, 237
  Hawaiian bread (elite), 212, 213
  maple pecan bread (elite), 120, 121
  orange-apple bread (transition), 110,
    111
  orange walnut bread (transition), 230,
    231
  prune walnut bread (elite), 250, 251
  pumpkin spice bread (elite), 222, 223
Nut butters, 270

Oat bran, 266
  bread (elite), 72, 73
  buckwheat oat bread (elite), 82, 83

Oat flour, 26–27
  buckwheat oat bread (elite), 82, 83
  oat bran bread (elite), 72, 73
Oatmeal (rolled oats), 26
  apple walnut bread (elite), 232, 233
  bread (transition), 60, 61
  oat bran bread (elite), 72, 73
  poppy seed bread (elite), 114, 115
Oats, 26–27
  health benefits of, 23
Oils, 19, 270–272
Old-fashioned wheat bread (transition),
  56, 57
Olive:
  green, and rosemary spread, 254–255
  and sweet red pepper topping, easy
    pizza sauce with, 168
Olive oil, 271, 272
  and wheat germ bread (elite), 158, 159
  100 percent whole wheat bread (elite),
    66, 67
Onion:
  bread, easy (transition), 126, 127
  caraway bread (elite), 178, 179
  roasted Italian vegetable spread, 257
  thyme bread (elite), 188, 189
Orange:
  apple bread (transition), 110, 111
  rolls (elite), 112, 113
  walnut bread (transition), 230, 231
Oven-baked challah (transition), 198, 199

Peach and honey jam, quick, 260
Peanut butter, 270
Pecan:
  apricot bread (elite), 116, 117
  carob date bread (elite), 242, 243
  maple bread (elite), 120, 121
Pepper:
  jalapeño corn bread (elite), 190, 191
  roasted Italian vegetable spread, 257
  sweet red, and olive topping, easy
    pizza sauce with, 168
Picnic breads, see Summer and picnic
    breads
Pilgrim bread (elite), 160, 161
Pizza, 162
  dough (transition), 166, 167
  sauce with sweet red pepper and olive
    topping, easy, 168
  summer tomato, 169

BREADMAN BREAD MIXES

All the taste with none of the trouble!

Breadman Bread Mixes, developed from the Breadman's family recipes specifically for the Breadman Automatic Bread Maker, bring you the nourishing goodness of the earth's finest organic grains. All you do is pour in the water, add the mix, and press start!

No nonsense nourishment!

Unlike typical store-bought ''Wheat Bread'' with its bran and germ removed, Breadman Bread Mixes provide all the nutrients of whole grains with their life-giving germ and cancer-fighting fiber intact.

No hydrogenated oils or shortening!

Breadman Bread Mixes are made only with natural pure oils—the oils highest in monounsaturated fats, such as canola, high-oleic sunflower and olive oil. These oils have been shown to lower levels of LDL (bad cholesterol), while maintaining levels of HDL (healthy cholesterol).

No additives, bromates, or so-called ''natural flavors'' like MSG!

Pure and simple, Breadman Bread Mixes proudly list every ingredient. You deserve to know what you're eating.

No refined sugars!

Breadman Bread Mixes are sweetened entirely with only the smallest amount of unrefined, unbleached sugars, such as Sucanat (organic evaporated cane juice) and pure organic barley malt.

Try all 6 deliciously healthy breads!

Low in calories and fat. High in complex carbohydrates, fiber, vitamins, and minerals. Few things in life are this nourishing, this satisfying, this easy!

Breadman Whole Wheat Bread Mix
Breadman Light Wheat Bread Mix
Breadman 7-Grain Bread Mix
Breadman Cinnamon-Raisin Bread Mix
Breadman Carob Date Nut Bread Mix
Breadman Caraway Rye Bread Mix

To Order These Bread Mixes Or For a Free Brochure,

CALL 1-800-800-8455

or write to:

The Breadman
655 South Orcas
Seattle, WA 98108

The **Breadman** Automatic Bread Machine
—the very best wholesome bread baker!

♦ The Breadman's very own bread machine, designed and developed to meet his exacting specifications.

♦ Cutting edge computer technology gives you delicious wholesome breads, consistently baked to perfection in as little as 2½ hours, with only 5 minutes of your time.

♦ Cycles for European, Fruit-and-Nut, and Wheat breads or Dough (ready for challah or cinnamon buns), let you create exactly the bread you want. And you can choose either a 1- or 1.5-pound loaf!

♦ Computer monitored cool-down cycle eliminates condensation as bread cools, ensuring perfectly crisp crusts for every bread every time.

♦ Automatic timer feature lets you decide when your bread will be ready, up to 12 hours after you set it. Wake up or come home to the delicious aroma of freshly baked bread!

♦ Built-in cover window invites you to relax and watch the entire bread-making process.

♦ **PLUS** with your **Breadman** order, you also get:
  * Video Operations Guide, featuring George Burnett, "The Breadman"
  * Healthy Whole Grain Bread Recipes & Menu Planner
  * 3 different Breadman Breadmixes for 3 delicious loaves of bread!

ALL THIS FOR ONLY $299.00

To Order Your New Breadman Or For a Free Brochure,

CALL 1-800-800-8455